400 Must-Have Words
for the TOEFL®

400 Must-Have Words
for the TOEFL®

Lynn Stafford-Yilmaz
Lawrence J. Zwier

McGraw-Hill

New York • Chicago • San Francisco • Lisbon
London • Madrid • Mexico City • Milan • New Delhi
San Juan • Seoul • Singapore • Sydney • Toronto

The McGraw·Hill Companies

1 2 3 4 5 6 7 8 9 0 DOC/DOC 0 9 8 7 6 5

ISBN 0-07-144328-2

This publication is designed to provide accurate and authoritative information in regard to the subject matter covered. It is sold with the understanding that neither the author nor the publisher is engaged in rendering legal, accounting, or other professional service. If legal advice or other expert assistance is required, the services of a competent professional person should be sought.

> —*From a declaration of principles jointly adopted by a committee of the American Bar Association and a committee of publishers.*

 This book is printed on recycled, acid-free paper containing a minimum of 50% recycled de-inked fiber.

McGraw-Hill books are available at special quantity discounts to use as premiums and sales promotions, or for use in corporate training programs. For more information, please write to the Director of Special Sales, Professional Publishing, McGraw-Hill, Two Penn Plaza, New York, NY 10121-2298. Or contact your local bookstore.

TOEFL® is a registered trademark of the Educational Testing Service (ETS). This publication is not endorsed or approved by ETS.

This book is dedicated to my late father, Richard J. Zwier, an intelligent, unselfish man.

And to my dear friend Sepideh Farsai, who developed a keen command of both the vocabulary and idioms of English.

Contents

Society

Money

Government and Justice

Relationships

Culture

Introduction

400 Must-Have Words for the TOEFL® will help you improve your score on the TOEFL test. In particular, this book will build your TOEFL vocabulary for the new Internet-based TOEFL of 2005.

This book is designed for ease of use as a self-study guide. Its chapters were written for easy completion in one sitting—about 25 minutes. *400 Must-Have Words* is also highly effective in the TOEFL-prep classroom.

Each chapter begins with a list of 10 target words. These words are defined and used in sample sentences. Usage tips are given for many words, as are any commonly used parts of speech related to the target word.

Following these definitions, the words are practiced in three exercises. TOEFL Prep I and TOEFL Prep II give straightforward practice in a variety of easy exercise styles. The last exercise, TOEFL Success, includes a TOEFL-style reading followed by one or two authentic TOEFL-style questions. Most TOEFL Success readings incorporate all 10 target words, and most also include an additional bonus structure. Each chapter ends with an answer key so you can check your work.

As an extra feature, this book includes a special front section called "Six Quick Hints for Success on the TOEFL®." These hints give general test-taking advice for TOEFL success.

This book was written by ELT professionals who help prepare students for the TOEFL test. Their selection of words for this book was based on extensive experience with the TOEFL test, information about the corpus (body of words) that is used in creating the actual TOEFL test, and TOEFL materials published by ETS, the creators of the TOEFL test.

400 Must-Have Words for the TOEFL® is the best book on the market to improve your vocabulary for the TOEFL test.

Six Quick Hints for Success on the TOEFL®

1. **Try to understand a reading or lecture as a whole.** Unlike earlier versions of the TOEFL, the new version tests whether you can see how ideas interact in a longer reading.

2. **Take notes.** Especially in the listening section, you will need notes to remember what you have heard. Note-taking will also help you concentrate. You can practice by taking notes of news stories, documentaries, or lectures.

3. **Study grammar in context, not by itself.** Unlike earlier versions of the TOEFL, the new version has no grammar section. Your knowledge of grammar is useful in helping you understand the readings and lectures, not in answering grammar-specific questions.

4. **Practice writing essays that express your opinion on a topic.** The writing section of the 2005 TOEFL includes questions asking for your opinion on various daily topics. These are timed. Practice writing under a time limit, shaping your thoughts into a well-rounded essay.

5. **Build up your academic vocabulary.** Your ability to comprehend reading passages rests largely on your academic vocabulary. Build your vocabulary by reading, making flash cards, and writing sentences using new words in context. A strong vocabulary will help you not only in your reading comprehension, but also in listening, writing, and speaking.

6. **Commit your attention to the test.** Some of the topics covered in the test may not actually interest you. Still, your focused energy will improve your test score. Agree with yourself not to think about other topics during the test. Force yourself to keep your attention on the tested material.

400 Must-Have Words
for the TOEFL®

Nature

Food Crops

Target Words

1. abandon	6. intensify
2. adversely	7. irrigation
3. aggregate	8. obtain
4. cultivation	9. photosynthesis
5. fertilize	10. precipitation

Definitions and Samples

1. **abandon** *v.* To leave; to give up

   To save their lives, the sailors had to **abandon** the sinking ship.

   Parts of speech abandonment *n*

2. **adversely** *adv.* In a harmful way; negatively

   Excessive rainfall early in the spring can **adversely** affect the planting of crops.

   Usage tips *Adversely* is often followed by *affect.*

   Parts of speech adversity *n*, adverse *adj*

3. **aggregate** *adj.* Gathered into or amounting to a whole

   It is impossible to judge last year's performance without knowing the **aggregate** sales numbers.

   Usage tips *Aggregate* is often followed by a term like *sum, total,* or *numbers.*

   Parts of speech aggregate *v*, aggregate *n*

4. **cultivation** *n.*   Preparing the land to grow crops; improvement for agricultural purposes

With the development of land **cultivation,** hunters and gatherers were able to settle in one place.

Parts of speech   cultivate *v*

5. **fertilize** *v.*   To supply with nourishment for plants by adding helpful substances to the soil

This farm **fertilizes** tomatoes more than any other crop.

Parts of speech   fertilizer *n,* fertilization *n*

6. **intensify** *v.*   To increase in power; to act with increased strength

Jacob's long absence **intensified** his certainty that he should marry Rose.

Parts of speech   intensification *n,* intense *adj*

7. **irrigation** *n.*   The supplying of water to dry land

In dry areas of the country, you can see ditches all over the farmland for **irrigation.**

Parts of speech   irrigate *v*

8. **obtain** *v.*   To gain possession of; to get

After a series of difficult interviews, he finally was able to **obtain** the job.

9. **photosynthesis** *n.*   The process by which green plants make their own food by combining water, salts, and carbon dioxide in the presence of light.

Oxygen is a by-product of the process of **photosynthesis.**

Parts of speech   photosynthesize *v*

10. **precipitation** *n.*   Water that falls to the Earth's surface

In the Pacific Northwest, the high level of **precipitation** ensures rich, green plant life.

TOEFL Prep I Complete each sentence by filling in the blank with the best word from the list. Change the form of the word if necessary. Use each word only once.

abandoned   *precipitation*   *cultivation*   *fertilize*   *photosynthesis*

1. Through _____, green plants create organic materials with the help of chlorophyll.

2. The coastal city gets half of its _____ during the months of January, February, and March.

3. Farmers use various methods of land _____.

4. When they heard the hull crack, all but two of the sailors _____ ship.

5. Inexperienced gardeners may not realize how important it is that they _____ their plants.

TOEFL Prep II Find the word or phrase that is closest in meaning to the opposite of each word in the left-hand column. Write the letter in the blank.

_____ 1. obtain   (a) weaken
_____ 2. intensify   (b) separate
_____ 3. irrigation   (c) lose
_____ 4. aggregate   (d) drainage
_____ 5. adversely   (e) positively

TOEFL Success Read the passage to review the vocabulary you have learned. Answer the questions that follow.

In countries like Niger and Mauritania, the *cultivation* of land has changed little in the past several centuries. Additionally, these countries' mono-modal rainfall pattern brings *precipitation* for only three months during the year. **As a result,** food production doesn't nearly meet demand.

> **Bonus Structure—**
> **As a result** *means* "therefore," "for this reason."

Several agencies and organizations have *intensified* their efforts to increase the productivity of land in these countries. They have introduced new strains of seed, improved *irrigation* techniques, and introduced new methods of *fertilization* and soil management. With ample sunlight for *photosynthesis* and modern *irrigation* techniques, sustainable farming techniques should allow farmers to boost *aggregate* production in order to meet demand.

Still, crop revitalization faces an unexpected <u>adversary</u>: institutional incompetence. Where crop specialists have convinced individual farmers to *abandon* old farming techniques in place of new, <u>they</u> can't readily *obtain* the governmental cooperation they need. The biggest hurdles are political corruption, incompetence, and the absence of a marketing infrastructure.

1. In this passage, the word <u>adversary</u> is closest in meaning to

   a. friend

   b. helper

   c. enemy

   d. leader

2. In the last paragraph, the word <u>they</u> refers to

   a. crop specialists

   b. farmers

   c. farming techniques

   d. adversaries

Lesson 1   Food Crops

    TOEFL Prep I   1. photosynthesis   2. precipitation   3. cultivation
      4. abandoned   5. fertilize
    TOEFL Prep II   1. c   2. a   3. d   4. b   5. e
    TOEFL Success   1. c   2. a

Disaster

Target Words

1. anticipate	6. flood
2. catastrophic	7. impact
3. collide	8. persevere
4. eruption	9. plunge
5. famine	10. unleash

Definitions and Samples

1. anticipate *v.*   To expect; to sense something before it happens

By placing sensors in earthquake-prone areas, scientists can **anticipate** some tremors in time to warn the public.

Parts of speech   anticipation *n*, anticipatory *adj*

2. catastrophic *adj.*   Extremely harmful; causing financial or physical ruin

The architect died in a **catastrophic** elevator accident.

Parts of speech   catastrophe *n*, catastrophically *adv*

3. collide *v.*   To come together with great or violent force

As usual, their holiday was ruined when their in-laws' views on politics **collided** with their own.

Parts of speech   collision *n*

4. eruption *n.*   A sudden, often violent, outburst

The **eruption** of Mount St. Helens in 1980 caused 57 deaths and immeasurable change to the face of the mountain.

Usage tips   *Eruption* is often followed by an *of* phrase.

Parts of speech   erupt *v*

5. famine *n.*   Severe hunger; a drastic food shortage

The potato **famine** in Ireland in the mid-nineteenth century caused large numbers of Irish people to emigrate to America.

6. flood *n.*   An overflowing of water; an excessive amount

The constant rain and poor drainage system caused a **flood** in town.

The political party sent out a **flood** of letters criticizing their opponents.

Parts of speech   flood *v*

7. impact *n.*   A strong influence

The speech about the importance of education made an **impact** on me.

Usage tips   *Impact* is usually followed by *on* or *of.*

Parts of speech   impact *v*

8. persevere *v.*   To keep going, despite obstacles or discouragement; to maintain a purpose

The hikers **persevered** despite the bad weather and the icy trail.

Parts of speech   persist *v,* persistent *adj*

9. plunge *v.*   To go down suddenly; to decrease by a great amount in a short time

He jumped off the diving board and **plunged** into the pool.

The value of the company's stock **plunged** after its chief executive was arrested.

Usage tips *Plunge* is often followed by an *into* phrase.

Parts of speech plunge *n*

10. **unleash** *v.* To release a thing or an emotion

When they saw the strange man on their property, they **unleashed** their dogs.

He is from such an unemotional family, he will never learn to **unleash** his feelings.

TOEFL Prep I Find the word or phrase that is closest in meaning to the opposite of each word in the left-hand column. Write the letter in the blank.

_____ 1. persevere
_____ 2. anticipate
_____ 3. famine
_____ 4. collide
_____ 5. catastrophic

(a) to pass by without hitting
(b) to give up
(c) to not see something coming
(d) harmless
(e) excess of food

TOEFL Prep II Circle the word that best completes each sentence.

1. Residents of Hawaii must accept the possibility of a volcanic (eruption / perseverance).
2. Years after the accident, she was finally able to (anticipate / unleash) her feelings of anger.
3. Houses along the river often face (famine / flooding) during the rainy season.
4. Many people think it is cruel to (collide / plunge) live lobsters into boiling water.
5. A well-written essay should make some kind of (catastrophe / impact) on its readers.

TOEFL Success   Read the passage to review the vocabulary you have learned. Answer the questions that follow.

Nature challenges humans in many ways, through disease, weather, and *famine*. For those living along the coast, one unusual phenomenon capable of *catastrophic* destruction is the tsunami (pronounced "tsoo-NAH-mee"). A tsunami is a series of waves generated in a body of water by an impulsive disturbance. Earthquakes, landslides, volcanic *eruptions*, explosions, and even the *impact* of meteorites can generate tsunamis. Starting at sea, a tsunami slowly approaches land, growing in height and losing energy through bottom friction and turbulence. Still, just like any other water waves, tsunamis *unleash* tremendous energy as they *plunge* onto the shore. They have great erosion potential, stripping beaches of sand, undermining trees, and *flooding* hundreds of meters inland. They can easily crush cars, homes, vegetation, and anything they *collide* with. To minimize the devastation of a tsunami, scientists are constantly trying to *anticipate* them more accurately and more quickly. Because many factors come together to produce a life-threatening tsunami, foreseeing them is not easy. **Despite this,** researchers in meteorology *persevere* in studying and predicting tsunami behavior.

Bonus Structure—
Despite this
means "even so;
regardless."

1. Which sentence best expresses the essential information of this passage?

    a. Tsunamis could become a new source of usable energy in the next hundred years.
    b. Tsunamis do more damage to the land than flooding.
    c. Tsunamis can have an especially catastrophic impact on coastal communities.
    d. Scientists can predict and track tsunamis with a fair degree of accuracy, reducing their potential impact.

2. In the first sentence, why does the author mention weather?

    a. because tsunamis are caused by bad weather
    b. because tsunamis are more destructive than weather phenomena
    c. as an example of a destructive natural force
    d. as an introduction to the topic of coastal storms

Lesson 2   Disaster

     TOEFL Prep I   1. b   2. c   3. e   4. a   5. d

     TOEFL Prep II   1. eruption   2. unleash   3. flooding   4. plunge

       5. impact

     TOEFL Success   1. c   2. c

Evolution and Migration

Target Words

1. adapt
2. diverse
3. evolve
4. feature
5. generation
6. inherent
7. migration
8. physical
9. process
10. survive

Definitions and Samples

1. **adapt** *v.* To adjust to the circumstances; to make suitable

   Dinosaurs could not **adapt** to the warmer temperatures.

   The teacher **adapted** the exercises for his more advanced students.

   Usage tips *Adapt* is often followed by *to*.

   Parts of speech adaptation *n*, adapter *n*, adaptable *adj*

2. **diverse** *n.* Various; showing a lot of differences within a group

   India is one of the most linguistically **diverse** countries in the world.

   Usage tips An *-ly* adverb (e.g., *linguistically*) often comes before *diverse*.

   Parts of speech diversify *v*, diversity *n*, diversification *n*

3. **evolve** *v.* To develop; to come forth

   Modern-day sharks **evolved** from their ancestor *Eryops*, which lived more than 200 million years ago.

Usage tips *Evolve* is often followed by *into* or *from.*

Parts of speech evolution *n*, evolutionist *n*

4. **feature** *n.* Part, characteristic

The best **feature** of this car is its heated seats.

Usage tips *Feature* is often followed by *of.*

Parts of speech feature *v*

5. **generation** *n.* A group of people born at about the same time

As older managers retired, a new **generation** of leaders took control of the company.

Usage tips Before *generation,* an adjective like *new, next, earlier,* or *older* is common. *Generation* is often followed by *of.*

Parts of speech generational *adj*

6. **inherent** *adj.* Naturally characteristic; always found within something, because it's a basic part of that thing

No job can be interesting all the time. Boredom is **inherent** in any kind of work.

Usage tips *Inherent* is often followed by *in.*

Parts of speech inherently *adv*

7. **migration** *n.* Movement from one place to another by a group of people or animals

The **migration** of farm workers from one state to the next depends primarily on the harvest.

Usage tips *Migration* is often followed by *to* or *from.*

Parts of speech migrate *v*, migrant *n*, migratory *adj*

8. **physical** *adj.* Related to the body; related to materials that can be seen or felt

Because of the shape of its throat, an ape does not have the **physical** ability to speak.

The mountains form a **physical** barrier between the west and the east.

Usage tips   *Physical* usually comes before the noun it describes.

Parts of speech   physically *adv*

9. **process** *n.*   A series of steps leading to a result

To get a good job, most people go through a long **process** of letter-writing and interviews.

Usage tips   *Process* is often followed by *of* plus the *-ing* form of a verb.

Parts of speech   proceed *v*, process *v*

10. **survive** *v.*   To continue living (despite some danger or illness)

After getting lost in the mountains, Gordon **survived** by eating wild plants and catching fish.

Usage tips   *Survive* is often followed by a phrase with *by*.

Parts of speech   survivor *n*, survival *n*

TOEFL Prep I   Find the word or phrase that is closest in meaning to the opposite of each word in the left-hand column. Write the letter in the blank.

_____ 1. physical	(a) not an integral part
_____ 2. migration	(b) stay the same
_____ 3. adapt	(c) die
_____ 4. inherent	(d) staying in one place
_____ 5. survive	(e) mental

TOEFL Prep II   Choose the word from the list that is closest in meaning to the underlined part of each sentence. Write it in the blank.

diverse   evolved   generation   process   survive

_____1. <u>Various</u> languages are spoken on the Indian subcontinent.

_____2. Making bread involves a <u>sequence of steps</u> that takes about three hours.

_____3. Few sea turtles <u>manage to live through</u> their first year of life.

_____4. This <u>age group</u> tends to support current educational policies.

_____5. Her thinking about economics has <u>changed slowly</u> in the last several months.

TOEFL Success   Read the passage to review the vocabulary you have learned. Answer the questions that follow.

The *migration* from Asia to North America across the Bering Strait (perhaps by land bridge) was a <u>monumental</u> event in human history. The *process* of overspreading the Americas took more than 1,000 years, or 30 *generations*. This might seem to confirm common sense—that slow travel was *inherent* in any great migration without wheeled vehicles across unknown terrain. **Further thought** shows that this process was remarkably fast—about 10 north-south miles per year, on average. The Americas were populated at an astounding pace, when one considers the *physical* limits of the human body and the physical

> *Bonus Structure—* **Further thought** *means "looking deeper; thinking more."*

features of the American continents. Legs of humans can move only so fast under the best of circumstances, and they work even slower over mountain passes or deserts. Populations spread through the *diverse* regions of the Americas (grasslands, eastern forests, coastal swamps) and needed to *adapt* to their new environments. The migrants' lifestyle had *evolved* over the years to that of professional nomads ensuring that they would find the resources needed to *survive*.

1. Which sentence best expresses the essential information in this passage?

    a. Human migration across the Bering Strait was remarkably slow.
    b. Physical limitations made migration across the Bering Strait almost impossible.
    c. Humans readily adapted to life in the Bering Strait.
    d. The migration through the Americas was surprisingly fast.

2. In this passage, the word <u>monumental</u> is closest in meaning to

    a. disastrous
    b. evolving
    c. important
    d. physical

Lesson 3   Evolution and Migration

TOEFL Prep I   1. e   2. d   3. b   4. a   5. c

TOEFL Prep II   1. diverse   2. process   3. survive   4. generation
    5. evolved

TOEFL Success   1. a   2. c

Petroleum Alternatives

Target Words

1. constraint   6. emission
2. contamination   7. extinction
3. deplete   8. reservoir
4. dispose of   9. shrink
5. elementally   10. stable

Definitions and Samples

1. **constraint** *n.*   Something that restricts thought or action

   The **constraints** of military life kept Eileen from seeing Private Morris more than once a month.

   Parts of speech   constrain *v*

2. **contamination** *n.*   Being made less clean by a germ or hazardous substance

   The **contamination** in the river came from the factory located just upstream.

   Parts of speech   contaminate *v*, contaminant *n*

3. **deplete** *v.*   To greatly decrease the supply of a resource or material

   The prolonged war **depleted** the country's national treasury.

   Parts of speech   depletion *n*

4. **dispose of** *v.*   To throw away; to get rid of; to kill

She **disposed of** her unwanted possessions before moving.

The tyrant cruelly **disposed of** all his enemies.

Usage tips   *Dispose of* should be learned as a unit. In this meaning, *dispose* does not occur without *of*.

Parts of speech   disposal *n,* disposable *adj*

5. **elementally** *adv.*   In terms of elements; basically

Elementally, coal and diamonds are the same.

Parts of speech   element *n,* elemental *adj*

6. **emission** *n.*   Sending out from a small space into the general environment; a substance discharged into the air

The Environmental Protection Agency regulates the **emission** of pollutants into the air.

Usage tips   *Emission* is usually followed by an *of* phrase.

Parts of speech   emit *v*

7. **extinction** *n.*   Complete disappearance; the end of existence

Human beings have caused the **extinction** of many other species.

Usage tips   *Extinction* implies an absolute end; an extinct thing cannot be brought back into existence.

Parts of speech   extinct *adj*

8. **reservoir** *n.*   A place where a liquid is collected and stored

Cult members threatened to poison the town's water **reservoir.**

Parts of speech   reserve *v*

9. **shrink** *v.*   To become reduced in size, amount, or value

If you dry your clothing on the "high heat" setting, they may **shrink.**

Parts of speech   shrinkage *n,* shrinkable *adj*

10. **stable** *adj.*   Firm and dependable; showing little change

He fell because the ladder wasn't **stable.**

Parts of speech   stability *n*, stably *adv*

TOEFL Prep I   Find the word that is closest in meaning to the opposite of each word in the left-hand column. Write the letter in the blank.

_____ 1. stable	(a) keep
_____ 2. contamination	(b) expand
_____ 3. extinct	(c) unsteady
_____ 4. dispose of	(d) existing
_____ 5. shrink	(e) purity

TOEFL Prep II   Circle the word that best completes each sentence.

1. The (constraints / contamination) of being in prison made her hate society even more.
2. A recognition that the Earth is round was one of the (elemental / shrunken) advances in thought during the time period.
3. Mother Teresa, who helped the poorest of the poor, had a great (disposal / reservoir) of love within her spirit.
4. Automobiles are responsible for some (emissions / extinction) of greenhouse gases.
5. By the end of the storm, the hikers had (depleted / reserved) even their emergency stores.

TOEFL Success   Read the passage to review the vocabulary you have learned. Answer the question that follows.

Human consumption of fossil fuels is expected to fully *deplete* the Earth's crude oil reserves by the year 2060. As underground *reservoirs* of oil continue to *shrink*, we have no choice but to find alternatives. **One promising source,** with much cleaner *emissions,* is called bio-diesel. Bio-

Bonus Structure— One promising source *signals the point of this paragraph.*

diesel is often made from soybean oil, although it can be made from any vegetable oil that is not *elementally* different from soy. Bio-diesel can even be made from used cooking oils that homes or restaurants would otherwise *dispose of*. Bio-diesel can be used without *constraint* in any vehicle that runs on diesel—no modifications are needed. Presently, diesel engines can take up to 20 percent soy in their soy-diesel blend. As the need for bio-diesel increases and the technology improves, we may soon witness the *extinction* of the fossil-fueled vehicle. This is good news for the planet, as bio-diesel is a more *stable* source of energy than petroleum, and it reduces *contamination* of our air and water.

An introductory sentence for a brief summary of the passage is provided below. Complete the summary by selecting the three answer choices that express the most important ideas in the passage. In each blank, write the letter of one of your choices.

Bio-diesel is a promising alternative to fossil fuels.
•
•
•

a. Humans have shown little self-restraint in their consumption of fossil fuels.
b. Underground reservoirs of oil will soon be depleted.
c. Bio-diesel burns cleaner than fossil fuels.
d. Bio-diesel comes from a more stable source than petroleum.
e. Restaurants can save disposal fees on used cooking oil.

Lesson 4   Petroleum Alternatives

TOEFL Prep I   1. c   2. e   3. d   4. a   5. b
TOEFL Prep II   1. constraint   2. elemental   3. reservoir   4. emission   5. deplete
TOEFL Success   a, c, d

Science

Time Efficiency

Target Words

1. adjust	6. maximize
2. arbitrary	7. parallel
3. denominator	8. proportion
4. exponentially	9. rate
5. infinitesimal	10. sequence

Definitions and Samples

1. **adjust** *v.*   To change; to get accustomed to something

   Travelers are advised to **adjust** their watches before arriving in the new time zone.

   Parts of speech   adjustment *n,* adjustable *adj*

2. **arbitrary** *adj.*   Chosen simply by whim or chance, not for any specific reason

   The decision to build a school in Blackberry Township was **arbitrary,** without any thought to future housing patterns.

   Parts of speech   arbitrate *v,* arbitrator *n,* arbitrarily *adv*

3. **denominator** *n.*   The number written below the line in a fraction

   In the fraction ½, the number 2 is the **denominator.**

   Usage tips   The phrase *lowest common denominator* means "the most basic and unsophisticated things that most people share."

   Parts of speech   denominate *v,* denomination *n,* denominational *adj*

4. **exponentially** *adv.*   At a very fast rate

In Turkey, the value of the lira has decreased **exponentially** in the last several decades.

Usage tips   *Exponentially* is taken from mathematics, where an exponent is a number indicating how many times something is multiplied by itself. For example, 4^3 contains the exponent "3," indicating $4 \times 4 \times 4$.

Parts of speech   exponent *n*, exponential *adj*

5. **infinitesimal** *adj.*   Immeasurably small

The number of contaminants in the water was **infinitesimal,** so the water was safe to drink.

Parts of speech   infinitesimally *adv*

6. **maximize** *v.*   To increase or make as great as possible

A coach helps each athlete **maximize** his or her potential.

Parts of speech   maximum *n*, maximum *adj*

7. **parallel** *adj.*   Being an equal distance apart everywhere

The street where I live runs **parallel** to the main road through town.

Usage tips   *Parallel* is often followed by *to.*

Parts of speech   parallel *n*, parallel *adv*

8. **proportion** *n.*   A part in relation to the whole

The average employee spends a large **proportion** of each workday answering e-mails.

Usage tips   *Proportion* is often followed by *of.*

Parts of speech   proportionate *adj*, proportionally *adv*

9. **rate** *n.*   The cost per unit of a good or service; the motion or change that happens in a certain time.

Postal **rates** in Japan are among the highest in the world.

Some grasses grow at the **rate** of one inch per day.

Parts of speech   rate *v*, rating *n*

10. **sequence** *v.*   To organize or arrange in succession

Volunteers have been asked to **sequence** the files and organize the boxes.

Parts of speech   sequence *n*, sequentially *adv*

TOEFL Prep I   Complete each sentence by filling in the blank with the best word from the list. Change the form of the word if necessary. Use each word only once.

adjust   arbitrary   denominator   infinitesimal   rate

1. Students felt that the exam was unfair and the grading system was rather _____.

2. The _____ of increase in prices made it difficult for people to afford basic goods.

3. Politicians promised great changes in the coming year, but any improvement in people's lives was _____.

4. She quickly overcame her culture shock and found it easy to _____ to the new country.

5. You can add two fractions that have the same _____.

TOEFL Prep II   Find the word or phrase that is closest in meaning to the opposite of each word in the left-hand column. Write the letter in the blank.

_____ 1. arbitrary	(a)	mix up
_____ 2. maximize	(b)	intersecting
_____ 3. sequence	(c)	minimize
_____ 4. infinitesimal	(d)	huge
_____ 5. parallel	(e)	planned out

TOEFL Success   Read the passage to review the vocabulary you have learned. Answer the questions that follow.

Time is, **as we all know,** money. Such valuation of time leads people to extreme efforts to *maximize* their use of time. Some people obsess over knowing the exact time. They buy clocks and watches that automatically *adjust* themselves over the Internet or by radio waves. These measurements allow them *infinitesimal* accuracy in dealing with time. Regardless of how one tracks time, most people share a common goal: They want to use time effectively. Since about 1982, this efficiency has increased *exponentially* each year, thanks to computers and their ability to multitask. In multitasking, a computer executes several different tasks in *parallel*. Rather than being set *arbitrarily,* each task is given a priority in the computer's operating system, and time is spent in *proportion* to the priority of the task. The computer executes different *sequences* of tasks at different clock cycles, thereby increasing the *rate* of output from a process.

> **Bonus Structure—**
> **As we all know**
> *is a writer's device*
> *for appealing to*
> *common knowledge.*

1. Why does the author mention computer multitasking in this article?
   a. because it is new
   b. because it measures time better than any clock
   c. because it helps people to arrange their activities sequentially
   d. because it is a good example of the efficient use of time

2. The underlined word *sequences* in the passage is closest in meaning to
   a. styles
   b. lengths
   c. orderings
   d. difficulty levels

Lesson 5   Time Efficiency

TOEFL Prep I   1. arbitrary   2. rate   3. infinitesimal   4. adjust
   5. denominator
TOEFL Prep II   1. e   2. c   3. a   4. d   5. b
TOEFL Success   1. d   2. c

Ancient Life

Target Words

1. accuracy
2. adjacent
3. compress
4. feasibly
5. gut

6. integrally
7. overlap
8. retain
9. seep
10. structure

Definitions and Samples

1. **accuracy** *n.*   Precision; exactness

   The research department checks all our articles for **accuracy** of facts before we print them.

   Usage tips   *Accuracy* is often followed by *of*.

   Parts of speech   accurate *adj*, accurately *adv*

2. **adjacent** *adj.*   Next to

   Even though the villages are **adjacent** to each other, their residents speak different languages.

   Usage tips   *Adjacent* is often followed by *to*.

   Parts of speech   adjacency *n*

3. **compress** *v.*   To press together

   To make the foundation stronger, they **compressed** the soil before pouring the concrete.

   Parts of speech   compression *n*, compressed *adj*

4. **feasibly** *adv.*   Practically; in a way that can work

Scientists can't **feasibly** bring energy from deep ocean currents to where it is needed—on land.

Parts of speech   feasibility *n*, feasible *adj*

5. **gut** *v.*   To empty or hollow out

In order to remodel the house, we must first **gut** it and throw away all the old fixtures.

Usage tips   *Gut* also means "the stomach of an animal"; this verb makes an image, that the inside of a building is like the inside of an animal.

Parts of speech   gut *n*, gutted *adj*

6. **integrally** *adv.*   In a whole or complete manner

Writing and spelling are taught **integrally** as part of the reading program.

Parts of speech   integrate *v*, integrity *n*, integral *n*, integral *adj*

7. **overlap** *v.*   To lie over part of something; to have elements in common

One of the two assistants will likely get fired, since most of their duties in the office **overlap.**

Parts of speech   overlap *n*

8. **retain** *v.*   To keep or hold

The rain fell so heavily that the banks of the river could not **retain** all the water.

Parts of speech   retainer *n*, retention *n*

9. **seep** *v.*   To pass slowly for a long time, as a liquid or gas might

As the containers rusted, the toxic waste **seeped** into the ground.

Usage tips   *Seep* is often followed by *into* or *through.*

10. **structure** *n.*   Something constructed, such as a building

   Most companies have a social **structure** that can't be understood by outsiders.

   Parts of speech   structure *v*, structural *adj*, structurally *adv*

TOEFL Prep I   Complete each sentence by filling in the blank with the best word from the list. Change the form of the word if necessary. Use each word only once.

accuracy   adjacent   feasibly   integrally   structure

1. She had no idea how they could _____ take a big vacation and remodel their house in the same year.

2. Daily meditation is used _____ with medication and massage as part of the recovery plan.

3. The rival politicians were raised in _____ counties.

4. If you build a _____ next to this river, you must be sure it is safe against floods.

5. Once he ran for public office, he understood the importance of checking public statements for _____.

TOEFL Prep II   Find the word or phrase that is closest in meaning to the opposite of each word in the left-hand column. Write the letter in the blank.

_____ 1. seep   (a) fill
_____ 2. gut   (b) separate
_____ 3. retain   (c) stay contained
_____ 4. compress   (d) loosen
_____ 5. overlap   (e) throw away

TOEFL Success   Read the passage to review the vocabulary you have learned. Answer the questions that follow.

Organic products from ancient life are an *integral* part of the Earth's resources, offering scientists a more *accurate* picture of ancient life-forms. One key to ancient life comes in the form of petrified matter. Petrifaction is a process that slowly turns the remains of a living object into stone. In this process, minerals *seep* into a mass of organic matter. After the organic matter has been replaced, a mineral version of the living object is left. Petrifaction often occurs in trees that are found *adjacent* to rivers, floodable areas, and volcanoes, which provide the mud or ash that initially covers the organic matter. Some pieces of petrified wood *retain* the original cellular *structure* of the wood and the grain can be easily seen. **Today**, it is *feasible* to petrify wood in a simple laboratory process.

Bonus Structure— In this context, **today** *means "at present; at this time in history."*

Fossils are another way that ancient life is preserved. Most fossils include an animal's hard parts, such as teeth and bones. One type of fossil, called a trace fossil, may also include eggs, tooth marks, contents of the *guts,* and fossil excrement. Some products from ancient life offer us more than scientific knowledge. One such product is coal, a solid fuel of plant origin. It develops over millions of years, during which swamp vegetation is <u>submerged in</u> water, depleted of oxygen, and covered by layers and layers of sand and mud. These *overlapping* layers settle with the Earth's movements and are *compressed* over time.

1. Which sentence best expresses the essential information of this passage?

    a. Preserved life-forms, including petrified matter and fossils, teach us about ancient life.

    b. The primary function for preserved life-forms is scientific discovery.

    c. Scientists try to replicate natural processes that preserve ancient life-forms.

    d. Ancient organic matter provides the most concentrated forms of energy known to humans.

2. In the passage, the words <u>submerged in</u> are closest in meaning to

    a. made wet

    b. completely covered

    c. adjacent to

    d. depleted of

Lesson 6   Ancient Life

   TOEFL Prep I   1. feasibly   2. integrally   3. adjacent
      4. structure   5. accuracy
   TOEFL Prep II   1. c   2. a   3. e   4. d   5. b
   TOEFL Success   1. a   2. b

Computers

Target Words

1. circulate	6. implement
2. corrode	7. innovative
3. derive	8. installation
4. detection	9. maintenance
5. expeditiously	10. simulation

Definitions and Samples

1. **circulate** *v.*   To move throughout an area or group; to move along a somewhat circular route

    The gossip **circulated** quickly through the small town.

    Blood **circulates** more quickly during physical exercise.

    Usage tips   *Circulate* is often followed by *through.*

    Parts of speech   circulation *n*

2. **corrode** *v.*   To be slowly weakened by chemical reactions

    Sitting in salt water, the old coins **corroded** and became very easy to break.

    Usage tips   A familiar kind of corrosion produces rust, the reddish coating on iron or steel that has been exposed to air and water.

    Parts of speech   corrosion *n*

3. **derive** *v.*   To come from, usually through a long, slow process

The Cyrillic alphabet was **derived** from the Greek alphabet.

Usage tips   *Derive* is often followed by *from.*

Parts of speech   derivation *n,* derivative *adj*

4. **detection** *n.*   Discovering something that cannot easily be found

With new medical technology, the **detection** of cancer is much easier nowadays.

Usage tips   *Detection* is often followed by an *of* phrase.

Parts of speech   detect *v,* detectable *adj*

5. **expeditiously** *adv.*   Quickly and efficiently

Using carrier pigeons, the military commanders exchanged messages **expeditiously.**

Parts of speech   expedite *v,* expedition *n,* expeditious *adj*

6. **implement** *v.*   To make use of; to carry out

Not until after the new software was installed could we **implement** the new filing system.

Parts of speech   implement *n,* implementation *n*

7. **innovative** *adj.*   Ahead of the times; novel

The **innovative** use of props and lighting drew many favorable comments.

Parts of speech   innovation *n*

8. **installation** *n.*   Setting something into position for use

Installation of the new software takes only four minutes.

Parts of speech   install *v*

9. **maintenance** *n.*   The act of keeping something in good condition

The only problem with living in such a big house is that it requires a lot of **maintenance.**

Parts of speech   maintain *v*

10. simulation *n.*   An imitation or representation

To test car safety, automobile makers study crash **simulations.**

Parts of speech   simulate *v,* simulator *n*

TOEFL Prep I   Circle the most likely meaning of the word part that is shared within each set of words.

1. circulate, circumnavigate, circuit

   The root *circ / circum* probably means

   a. around
   b. broken
   c. fair
   d. straight

2. innovative, novel, renovate

   The root *nov* probably means

   a. clear
   b. old
   c. new
   d. sweet

3. installation, implement, imprison

   The prefix *in-/im-* probably means

   a. aside
   b. behind
   c. in
   d. out

TOEFL Prep II   Circle the word that best completes each sentence.

1. Please make sure this information (circulates / derives) throughout the office quickly.
2. The (installation / simulation) of the new telephones took three days.
3. In order to stay on schedule, we need to complete this project as (expeditiously / innovatively) as possible.

4. The smuggler moved cautiously through the airport to avoid (detection / maintenance).

5. Years of neglect had caused the building's water pipes to (corrode / implement).

TOEFL Success   Read the passage to review the vocabulary you have learned. Answer the questions that follow.

As dependence on computers increases, so does the need for technical support. From *installation* of software to *detection* of viruses, computers require constant vigilance. Most larger companies find it most *expeditious* to maintain in-house computer staff. Many smaller companies, however, can't fund their own full-time, in-house technical help. Instead, many of them assign the task of computer *maintenance* to a current employee who may not have any formal training. Rather, these "computer buffs" have *derived* their skills through practice and self-training. These self-appointed tech specialists, however, often cannot solve bigger problems. What's more, they may see their office relations *corrode* when they are swamped with basic user questions that they simply don't have time to address. For these reasons, many small companies choose to employ a freelance technical assistant who *circulates* among clients on an as-needed basis. With their professional training, these consultants may propose *innovative* solutions to users' unique needs, which could vary from tracking inventory to *simulating* mechanized processes. They can *implement* new programs, train personnel, and escape the workplace before being asked, "How can I cut this file and paste it somewhere else?"

1. Which sentence best expresses the essential information of this passage?

    a. Larger companies are better off using freelance technical consultants.

    b. Computer maintenance and troubleshooting cuts into employee productivity.

    c. Self-trained technical support personnel are often as effective as trained professionals.

    d. Smaller companies may benefit from hiring occasional technical support.

2. The article implies that the question *How do I cut and paste a file?* is

   a. too basic to require professional attention
   b. a good question to give to in-house tech support
   c. appropriate for a freelancer to address
   d. a good topic for a training program

Lesson 7   Computers

TOEFL Prep I 1. a 2. c 3. c
TOEFL Prep II 1. circulate 2. installation 3. expeditiously
    4. detection 5. corrode
TOEFL Success 1. d 2. a

Energy

Target Words

1. combustion
2. component
3. convey
4. discretely
5. nucleus

6. permeate
7. rotate
8. solar
9. source
10. trigger

Definitions and Samples

1. **combustion** *n.*   The process of burning

   When air quality is poor, **combustion** of materials in a fireplace is prohibited.

   Usage tips   *Combustion* is often followed by *of*.

   Parts of speech   combust *v*, combustible *adj*

2. **component** *n.*   One part of a system or whole

   Their home theater system has a number of separate **components**.

   Usage tips   *Component* is often followed or preceded by *of*.

3. **convey** *v.*   To transport from one place to another; to transmit or make known

   A messenger **conveyed** the prince's letter to the commander of the army.

The worst part about being a doctor was when she had to **convey** bad news to a family.

Parts of speech   conveyance *n,* conveyor *n*

4. **discretely** *adv.*   Separately; distinctly

In order to understand how the engine worked, each component needed to be studied **discretely.**

Parts of speech   discrete *adj*

5. **nucleus** *n.*   A central or essential part around which other parts are gathered; a core

The **nucleus** of many European cities is the town square.

Usage tips   *Nucleus* is often followed by *of.*

Parts of speech   nuclear *adj*

6. **permeate** *v.*   To spread or flow throughout; to pass through or penetrate

The smell of cooking **permeated** the entire apartment building.

Parts of speech   permeation *n*

7. **rotate** *v.*   To turn around; to take turns in sequence

The planet **rotates** on its axis once every 14 Earth days.

The children **rotate** classroom responsibilities on a weekly basis.

Parts of speech   rotation *n*

8. **solar** *adj.*   Of, or relating to, the sun

The ancient society kept time with a **solar** calendar.

9. **source** *n.*   The point of origin or creation

The reporter was unable to identify the **source** of the information for his story.

Parts of speech   source *v*

10. **trigger** *v.*   To set off or initiate

I was certain any mention of politics would **trigger** a big argument.

Parts of speech   trigger *n*

TOEFL Prep I   Complete each sentence by filling in the blank with the best word from the list. Change the form of the word if necessary. Use each word only once.

combustion   convey   permeate   source   trigger

1. It is often difficult to _____ the meaning of a poem to a large audience.

2. The _____ of the gossip was someone inside this office.

3. Her bad mood that day _____ the atmosphere in the laboratory.

4. The internal _____ engine revolutionized the way automobiles run.

5. A cigarette _____ the explosion.

TOEFL Prep II   Find the word or phrase that is closest in meaning to each word in the left-hand column. Write the letter in the blank.

_____ 1. rotate
_____ 2. solar
_____ 3. component
_____ 4. discretely
_____ 5. nucleus

(a) separately, as an individual part
(b) spin on an axis
(c) sun
(d) center
(e) part

TOEFL Success   Read the passage to review the vocabulary you have learned. Answer the questions that follow.

Most of the electricity in the United States is produced in steam turbines. There are many *discrete* steps in this process. In a steam turbine, *combustion* of coal, petroleum, or natural gas heats water to make steam. The steam *rotates* a shaft that is connected to a generator that produces electricity. Finally, that electricity is converted by a <u>transformer</u> and *conveyed* from the turbine to its place of use. Many *sources* can provide energy to heat the water in a steam turbine. Coal is primary, producing 51 percent of the country's electricity. Another common way to heat water for steam turbines is through *nuclear* power. In nuclear fission, atoms of uranium fuel are hit by neutrons, *triggering* a continuous chain of fission that releases heat. In 2001, nuclear power generated 21 percent of the electricity in the United States. *Solar* power produces less than 1 percent of the United States' electricity needs, because it is not regularly available and harnessing it is more expensive than using fossil fuels. Dependence on electricity *permeates* daily life in the United States. **Still,** few people are aware of the many *components* of electricity production.

*Bonus Structure—In this context, **still** means "even so; despite this."*

1. What does the author say about solar power?

   a. It produces more electricity than any other source.
   b. It is a relatively small source of energy for heating water in steam turbines.
   c. Electricity producers are trying to use it more regularly.
   d. Researchers are trying to make it cheaper to use.

2. In the passage, the word <u>transformer</u> probably refers to a

   a. truck
   b. generator that produces electricity
   c. type of turbine
   d. device that changes electric currents

Lesson 8 Energy

TOEFL Prep I   1. convey   2. source   3. permeated
       4. combustion   5. triggered
TOEFL Prep II   1. b   2. c   3. e   4. a   5. d
TOEFL Success   1. b   2. d

Mind and Body

Memory

Target Words

1. acquisition	6. indisputable
2. anomaly	7. intervene
3. consciously	8. intuitively
4. degrade	9. recede
5. gap	10. retrieve

Definitions and Samples

1. **acquisition** *n.* The act of taking possession of something

   Our recent **acquisition** of over 2,000 books makes ours the biggest library in the region.

   Usage tips *Acquisition* is often followed by *of.*

   Parts of speech acquire *v*

2. **anomaly** *n.* Something unusual

   White tigers get their beautiful coloring from a genetic **anomaly.**

3. **consciously** *adv.* With awareness of one's actions

   He may have hurt her feelings, but he never would have done so **consciously.**

   Parts of speech consciousness *n,* conscious *adj*

4. **degrade** *v.*   To reduce in value or strength

The roads in cold or wet areas of the United States **degrade** faster than those in warm, sunny regions.

Parts of speech   degradation *n,* degradable *adj*

5. **gap** *n.*   Opening; a big difference in amount or quality

The small **gap** between the walls in the old house caused cold drafts to come in.

6. **indisputable** *adj.*   Beyond doubt; unquestionable

The members of the jury found her guilty because they found the facts of the case **indisputable.**

Parts of speech   indisputably *adv*

7. **intervene** *v.*   To come between

A good mediator **intervenes** only as much as necessary to settle a dispute between other parties.

Parts of speech   intervention *n*

8. **intuitively** *adv.*   By means of a natural sense about things that are hard to observe

Many mothers know **intuitively** when something is wrong with their children.

Parts of speech   intuition *n,* intuitive *adj*

9. **recede** *v.*   To move back or away from

After the age of 30, his hairline began to **recede** further back from his forehead.

Parts of speech   recession *n,* recessive *adj*

10. **retrieve** *v.*   To bring or get back

Most dogs can be trained to **retrieve** objects that their owners have thrown.

Parts of speech   retriever *n,* retrievable *adj*

TOEFL Prep I   Find the word or phrase that is closest in meaning to the opposite of each word in the left-hand column. Write the letter in the blank.

_____ 1. degrade	(a) stay out of a dispute
_____ 2. anomaly	(b) improve
_____ 3. recede	(c) questionable
_____ 4. intervene	(d) the norm
_____ 5. indisputable	(e) come forward

TOEFL Prep II   Circle the word that best completes each sentence.

1. A huge (anomaly / gap) between the wealthy and the working class often leads to social unrest.
2. The new computers enable us to (intervene / retrieve) information more quickly.
3. Although she wasn't qualified for the job, she (indisputably / intuitively) felt that she should apply.
4. When he joined the military, he did not expect the officers to (degrade / recede) him.
5. The art in the foyer was an important (acquisition / consciousness) for the museum.

TOEFL Success   Read the passage to review the vocabulary you have learned. Answer the question that follows.

Like other functions of the human mind, perception and memory are imperfect. When we tell a story about something that we witnessed, we may *intuitively* believe that our recollection is accurate. However, several factors bias our memories of events. To study this *anomaly,* let us look at the three steps of memory creation: *acquisition* of memory, storing of memory, and *retrieval.* At every stage of memory formation, distortion can occur. At the first stage, acquisition of memory, events are perceived and bits of information are prepared for storage in the brain. However, it is impossible for us to remember every single thing we observe. Through processes that are both *conscious* and unconscious, people determine which details they will focus on.

In its second stage, storage, memories can become further distorted. Over time, our memories *degrade,* as we forget portions of events. To compensate, we may even creatively fill in the *gap* created by the *recession* of long-term memory. Additionally, an individual's memory can be altered during the storage stage by *intervening* occurrences, which can be subconsciously combined with previously stored memories. Last but not least, we search our memory to locate information. During recall, emotion also seems to play a part in memory distortion. **In sum,** our memories may not be the *indisputable* source of information that we would like them to be.

> **Bonus Structure—**
> **In sum** *means "to summarize; to give a short version of what has been stated."*

An introductory sentence for a brief summary of the passage is provided below. Complete the summary by selecting the three answer choices that express the most important ideas in the passage. In each blank, write the letter of one of your choices.

Memory provides an imperfect record of events.
•
•
•

a. People purposefully present a slanted version of events.
b. Memories can be altered at any point in memory creation.
c. People naturally cannot recall everything they observe.
d. Memories are an indisputable source of fact.
e. Time and emotion contribute to memory degradation.
f. Past occurrences often displace current memories.

Lesson 9 Memory

TOEFL Prep I   1. b   2. d   3. e   4. a   5. c
TOEFL Prep II   1. gap   2. retrieve   3. intuitively   4. degrade
    5. acquisition
TOEFL Success   b, c, e

Spirituality

Target Words

1. agnostic
2. animism
3. atheist
4. be inclined to
5. contemplate
6. deify
7. ecclesiastical
8. exalt
9. pious
10. sacrifice

Definitions and Samples

1. **agnostic** *adj.*   Believing that humans cannot know whether there is a god

   His devoutly Christian parents had problems with his **agnostic** beliefs.

   Parts of speech   agnostic *n*, agnosticism *n*

2. **animism** *n.*   The belief that natural objects, such as trees, have souls

   Desert cultures that practice **animism** often believe that winds contain spirits.

   Parts of speech   animistic *adj*

3. **atheist** *n.*   One who does not believe in the existence of a supreme being

   He argued that his scientific training made it impossible for him to be anything but an **atheist.**

   Parts of speech   atheistic *adj*

4. **be inclined to** *v.*   To favor an opinion or a course of action

He couldn't say which candidate he favored, but he had always **been inclined to** vote Republican.

Parts of speech   incline *n*, inclination *n*

5. **contemplate** *v.*   To consider thoughtfully

If you **contemplate** each step for so long, we will never complete this project on time.

Parts of speech   contemplation *n*, contemplative *adj*

6. **deify** *v.*   To worship as a god

When people **deify** the leader of their country, the leader is able to abuse power more easily.

Parts of speech   deity *n*

7. **ecclesiastical** *adj.*   Relating to a church

He was looking specifically for a university where he could study **ecclesiastical** history.

Parts of speech   ecclesiastic *n*, ecclesiastically *adv*

8. **exalt** *v.*   To praise or honor

He would often **exalt** the virtues of his new wife.

Parts of speech   exaltation *n*

9. **pious** *adj.*   Having or exhibiting religious reverence

Sometimes she was so **pious** that the rest of us felt like heathens.

Parts of speech   piousness *n*, piety *n*, piously *adv*

10. **sacrifice** *v.*   Anything offered to a deity as a religious thanksgiving; giving up something in order to have something more valuable later on

Every harvest time, the Fadeloni people **sacrificed** vegetables to their gods as a show of thanks.

In order to succeed in his career, he had to **sacrifice** his private life and his leisure time.

Parts of speech   sacrifice *n*, sacrificial *adj*, sacrificially *adv*

TOEFL Prep I   Complete each sentence by filling in the blank with the best word or phrase from the list. Change the form of the word if necessary. Use each word or phrase only once.

be inclined to   contemplate   deify   exalted   sacrifice

1. Traditionally, the Camerian society _____ its leaders, considering them to be sent from the land of the gods.

2. To do well in his university courses, he had to _____ a lot of his personal time.

3. The generation of American leaders known as "the Founders" are _____ by many scholars for their wisdom and courage.

4. She knew she would always _____ agree with what her mother said, so she struggled to remain unbiased.

5. The human resources department _____ whether they should let Mary go.

TOEFL Prep II   Circle the likely meaning of the word part that is shared within each set of words.

1. animism, animal, animation

   The root *anima* probably means

   a. color
   b. death
   c. many
   d. life

2. atheistic, amoral, apathetic

The prefix *a* probably means

a. not
b. loving
c. excessive
d. surely

TOEFL Success   Read the passage to review the vocabulary you have learned. Answer the questions that follow.

In Russia, several religions coexist, including Christianity, Judaism, Islam, and *animism*. The most common religion is Christianity, and most Christians are members of the Russian Orthodox Church. The Church has existed for over 1,000 years, surviving even the official *atheism* of the Soviet era and the *agnosticism* that may have been even more prominent at the time. During the communist years, many Russians who practiced Orthodoxy *sacrificed* career and educational opportunities. The tenacity of Russian Orthodoxy may explain why even nonreligious Russians *are inclined to* call themselves Russian Orthodox. That same staying power drives the Church today, which is run by Aleksey II of Moscow. Born Aleksey Mikhailovich Ridiger, the future patriarch was from a very *pious* family. As a boy, Aleksey was often taken by his parents on their annual pilgrimages, when he most certainly began *contemplation* of the religious way of life he was to choose. **As patriarch,** Aleksey is *exalted* in the Church governance, but he is not *deified*. Aleksey has published articles on Church history and peacemaking in both the *ecclesiastical* and secular press, broadening the Church's image both in Russia and abroad.

Bonus Structure—Here **As patriarch** *means "while working in the position of church leader."*

1. Which sentence best expresses the essential information of this passage?

a. The Russian Orthodox Church was banned under Soviet control.
b. Few Russians believe in a god.
c. Aleksey II has updated the church's image.
d. The Russian Orthodox Church has a long history of strong membership in Russia.

2. According to the passage, Aleksey II of Moscow is

   a. a god

   b. a high church official

   c. a secular leader

   d. an atheist

Lesson 10   Spirituality

TOEFL Prep I   1. deifies   2. sacrifice   3. exalted   4. be inclined to   5. contemplated

TOEFL Prep II   1. d   2. a

TOEFL Success   1. d   2. b

Illness

Target Words

1. aggravate
2. decrepit
3. disease
4. fatally
5. forensics

6. persist
7. prognosis
8. terminal
9. vein
10. wound

Definitions and Samples

1. **aggravate** *v.*   To make worse; to anger or intensify

    Running will **aggravate** your sore knees.

    Parts of speech   aggravation *n*

2. **decrepit** *adj.*   Weakened or worn out because of age, illness, or excessive use

    The once-beautiful building was now dirty, **decrepit,** and roofless.

3. **disease** *n.*   An unhealthful condition caused by an infection or a long-term physical problem

    Thanks to developments in medicine, many once-fatal **diseases** can now be cured.

4. **fatally** *adv.*   Causing death or disaster

    The soldier was **fatally** wounded in the battle.

    Parts of speech   fatality *n*, fatal *adj*

5. **forensics** *n.*   The use of science and technology to investigate facts in criminal cases

Advances in the study of **forensics** have made it much easier to identify criminals from very small traces of evidence.

Parts of speech   forensic *adj*

6. **persist** *v.*   To continue to exist; to hold to a purpose, despite any obstacle

If your symptoms **persist,** you should go see a doctor.

Lola **persisted** in her efforts to become a lawyer.

Parts of speech   persistence *n*, persistent *adj*

7. **prognosis** *n.*   An educated guess of how something will develop, especially a disease

The room fell silent when the doctor gave Senator Grebe a grim **prognosis** of months of treatment.

8. **terminal** *adj.*   Located at an end; approaching death

The cancer ward at the hospital held both **terminal** and recovering patients.

Parts of speech   terminate *v*, terminally *adv*

9. **vein** *n.*   Any of the tubes that form a branching system, especially those that carry blood to the heart

She became fascinated with human anatomy, especially when she learned how **veins** transport oxygen.

10. **wound** *v.*   To inflict an injury on

Sometimes he didn't realize his sharp humor could **wound** as well as entertain.

Parts of speech   wound *n*

TOEFL Prep I   Choose the word from the list that is closest in meaning to the underlined part of each sentence. Write it in the blank.

disease   fatal   persist   prognosis   wound

_____ 1. He sustained a serious <u>injury</u> in the war, so he was sent home immediately.

_____ 2. Her <u>sickness</u> was so rare, doctors weren't certain how to treat it.

_____ 3. His motto was to <u>keep trying</u>, no matter what happened.

_____ 4. The medical staff could not know for sure whether the treatment would work, but they made a confident <u>prediction</u> that the patient would recover.

_____ 5. The airplane crash was tragic, killing many people immediately and inflicting injuries on others that would eventually prove <u>deadly</u>.

TOEFL Prep II Next to each definition, write the word that most closely fits it.

aggravate   *decrepit*   *forensics*   *terminal*   *vein*

_____ 1. the science involved in solving crimes

_____ 2. a vessel for carrying blood

_____ 3. to make worse

_____ 4. unable to be cured

_____ 5. in very bad condition

TOEFL Success Read the passage to review the vocabulary you have learned. Answer the questions that follow.

The man was *decrepit.* With high blood pressure, cancer, and liver *disease,* he *aggravated* his situation by smoking. His *prognosis* was death. His advanced lung cancer was *terminal,* and his family members knew that he would pass away soon. So no one was surprised to find him dead on that sharp winter Thursday, no one, that is, except one sharp-eyed detective, who noticed the bedroom window ajar on the morning of the old man's death. Would a *fatally* ill person be likely to sleep with the window open on a freezing cold night?

This question occupied *forensic* specialists from the medical examiner's office. There, an autopsy revealed an unlikely <u>wound</u> on the victim's thigh. Such a wound could easily have been inflicted by someone administering medicine . . . or poison. From there, the poison could travel through the *veins,* shutting down vital organs and causing death within seconds.

Indeed, the death turned out to be murder in the first degree. Criminal investigators *persisted* in their questioning of friends and family, only later finding the motive: money. Two distant relatives who stood to <u>inherit</u> large sums from the old man's estate plotted the death, believing that the old man's death would not be questioned.

> *Bonus Structure—* **Indeed** *indicates that an idea in an earlier paragraph was actually true.*

1. Why does the author mention a <u>wound</u>?

   a. The wound caused the death.
   b. It was evidence of a struggle.
   c. It was suspicious.
   d. It was predictable, considering the man's disease.

2. In the passage, the word <u>inherit</u> is closest in meaning to

   a. lose
   b. gain
   c. earn
   d. want

Lesson 11   Illness

TOEFL Prep I   1. wound   2. disease   3. persist   4. prognosis
   5. fatal
TOEFL Prep II   1. forensics   2. vein   3. aggravate   4. terminal
   5. decrepit
TOEFL Success   1. c   2. b

Surgery

Target Words

1. anesthesia
2. augment
3. certifiably
4. complication
5. cure

6. implant
7. inject
8. obese
9. procedure
10. scar

Definitions and Samples

1. **anesthesia** *n.* Techniques for reducing sensation and feeling, especially to control pain

   The Civil War was the first American war when **anesthesia** was widely used in surgery on soldiers.

   Usage tips *Anesthesia* and *anesthetic* are often used interchangeably.

   Parts of speech anesthetic *n, adj*

2. **augment** *v.* To make bigger or better by adding to

   In some types of popular cosmetic surgery people **augment** parts of their bodies.

   The college **augmented** its course offerings because students complained that there were too few choices.

   Parts of speech augmentation *n*

3. **certifiably** *adv.*   In a manner that is officially recognized

He couldn't be institutionalized until he was declared **certifiably** insane.

Parts of speech   certify *v*, certification *n*, certificate *n*, certifiable *adj*

4. **complication** *n.*   A factor that makes something more difficult or complex

The surgeons could not easily stop the bleeding because of **complications** related to the patient's diabetes.

Parts of speech   complicate *v*

5. **cure** *v.*   To restore to health

They say laughter can help **cure** many illnesses.

Parts of speech   cure *n*

6. **implant** *v.*   To set in firmly; to insert in the body surgically

The actress had cheek **implants** to make her face look fuller.

Parts of speech   implantation *n*

7. **inject** *v.*   To insert a liquid by means of a syringe

The doctor used a needle to **inject** the medicine slowly into her arm.

Parts of speech   injection *n*

8. **obese** *adj.*   Excessively overweight

More Americans are **obese** now because U.S. culture encourages overeating and discourages exercise.

Parts of speech   obesity *n*

9. **procedure** *n.*   A specific way of performing or doing something

The flight attendant explained the emergency evacuation **procedure**.

Parts of speech   proceed *v*, procedural *adj*

10. **scar** *n.*   A mark on the skin left after a wound has healed; a lasting sign of damage, either mental or physical

The surgery was successful, but it left a large **scar** across her abdomen.

Parts of speech   scar *v*

TOEFL Prep I   For each word, choose the word or phrase that has the most similar meaning. Write the letter of your choice on the line.

1. scar   _____
   (a) bandage   (b) mark   (c) shine   (d) cover

2. augment   _____
   (a) take away   (b) discuss   (c) use   (d) add to

3. complication _____
   (a) added difficulty   (b) improved performance
   (c) method of training   (d) prediction about results

4. obese   _____
   (a) attractive   (b) healthy   (c) very overweight   (d) high

5. cure   _____
   (a) heal   (b) study   (c) diagnose   (d) tie up

TOEFL Prep II   Circle the word that best completes each sentence.

1. The (procedure / scar) to prepare for the surgery took four hours.
2. Only seriously (certifiable / obese) people should get their stomachs surgically reduced.
3. He almost died during the operation because the doctors did not give him the right kind of (anesthesia / complication).
4. Doctors are now able to (cure / implant) many types of sickness that were usually fatal in the past.
5. Before (augmenting / injecting) a painkiller, the dentist rubbed cloves on the woman's gums to numb them.

TOEFL Success   Read the passage to review the vocabulary you have learned. Answer the questions that follow.

Since 1992, the number of cosmetic surgery *procedures* has risen 175 percent in the United States. Two of the most popular are liposuction and breast *augmentation*. In liposuction, the doctor *inserts* a small tube into the skin that sucks fat from the body. And while it may sound easy, it isn't. Liposuction is so painful that people are often given *anesthesia*. **What's more,** liposuction is not really a *cure* for *obesity*. Rather, it should be used when diet and exercise do not reduce fat in certain "trouble spots." Another common cosmetic procedure is breast aug-

> *Bonus Structure—*
> **What's more**
> *means "in addition;*
> *even more*
> *importantly."*

mentation. In this procedure, an *implant* is inserted through the armpit, making the breasts appear larger. Breast augmentation usually leaves only a small *scar*. Some common *complications* include the effects of anesthesia, infection, swelling, redness, bleeding, and pain. To reduce these risks, consumers are advised to be sure that their surgeon is board-*certified*.

1. Which sentence best expresses the essential information of this passage?

   a. Cosmetic surgery is dangerous.
   b. Many people do not have cosmetic surgery because of the pain.
   c. Cosmetic surgery is increasing in popularity in the United States.
   d. Breast reduction is almost as popular as breast augmentation.

2. In the underlined sentence, *trouble spots* refers to

   a. places where people are commonly overweight
   b. methods of exercise that aren't effective
   c. parts of the body where liposuction doesn't work
   d. specific areas on the body where fat is hard to minimize

Lesson 12   Surgery

TOEFL Prep I   1. b   2. d   3. a   4. c   5. a
TOEFL Prep II   1. procedure   2. obese   3. anesthesia   4. cure
   5. injecting
TOEFL Success   1. c   2. d

LESSON 13

Ghosts

Target Words

1. astrological
2. divination
3. haunt
4. horror
5. intermediary
6. invoke
7. meditate
8. phantom
9. psychic
10. self-perpetuating

Definitions and Samples

1. **astrological** *adj.*   Related to the study of the position of stars, the sun, and the planets in the belief that they influence earthly events

   Every day, Mona read her **astrological** forecast in the newspaper, and she was careful if the horoscope predicted trouble.

   Parts of speech   astrology *n*, astrologer *n*, astrologically *adv*

2. **divination** *n.*   Foretelling the future by finding patterns in physical objects

   In Turkey, women offer **divinations** by reading the dregs from a coffee cup.

   Parts of speech   divine *v*

3. **haunt** *v.*   To continually appear (in the form of a ghost) in the same place or to the same person

Some say the ghost of Princess Hilda **haunts** this castle, appearing as a headless form while she plays the piano.

The pictures of children dying in war have **haunted** me for a long time.

4. **horror** *n.* Strong fear mixed with disgust

On Halloween night, all the **horror** movies were rented out.

Parts of speech horrify *v,* horrific *adj*

5. **intermediary** *n.* Acting as an agent between people or things

The plaintiff's lawyer suggested that they hire an **intermediary** to help them discuss their case.

Usage tips *Intermediary* comes from the Latin words meaning "between the ways."

6. **invoke** *v.* To call on for support

In many religions, believers **invoke** their god by holding out their hands.

Parts of speech invocation *n*

7. **meditate** *v.* To reflect; to think quietly and deeply for a long time

Every morning, the monks **meditated** for three hours in complete silence.

Parts of speech meditation *n*

8. **phantom** *n.* A dimly visible form, usually thought to be the spirit of a dead person, a sunken ship, etc.

Many visitors reported seeing a **phantom** who appeared around the lake.

Usage tips *Phantom* originates in a word meaning "dream"; like a dream, a phantom leaves an observer wondering whether it's real or not.

9. **psychic** *adj.*   Relating to the supposed ability of the human mind to sense things that cannot be observed

The governor's assistant claimed to have unique **psychic** abilities enabling him to read people's minds.

Parts of speech   psychic *n*, psychically *adv*

10. **self-perpetuating** *adj.*   Having the power to renew oneself for an indefinite period of time

It is difficult to escape from a lie, as they are often **self-perpetuating**.

Parts of speech   self-perpetuation *n*

TOEFL Prep I   For each word, choose the word or phrase that has the most similar meaning. Write the letter of your choice on the line.

1. divination   _____
    (a) demand   (b) prediction   (c) problem   (d) route

2. haunt   _____
    (a) dry out   (b) fail to show up
    (c) continue to disturb   (d) search desperately

3. meditate   _____
    (a) clarify   (b) expose   (c) purge   (d) think

4. invoke   _____
    (a) call   (b) cry   (c) inspire   (d) reject

5. psychic   _____
    (a) empty   (b) mental   (c) powerful   (d) vague

TOEFL Prep II   Circle the word that best completes each sentence.

1. The leaders of the religious group are said to have (astrological / psychic) powers that allow them to move objects just by the power of their thoughts.

2. For years after the earthquake, she was disturbed by the (haunting / self-perpetuating) memories of destruction.
3. The boys told their new friend that they had seen (intermediaries / phantoms) in the cemetery at night.
4. During the scuffle, the citizens were prepared to (invoke / meditate) the right of citizen's arrest because no police officers were present.
5. Her (divination / horror) of the results of their meeting impressed even the nonbelievers.

TOEFL Success   Read the passage to review the vocabulary you have learned. Answer the questions that follow.

Some say that sailors are a superstitious group. Long nights of watching stars predispose them to a belief in *astrology*. Long periods of isolation lead them to believe in *psychic* phenomena that others would laugh at. This may explain sailors' frequent reports of seeing *phantom* ships. From the Gulf of Mexico, across the Atlantic, and to the South China Sea, sailors often claim that such vessels *haunt* the seas. One of the most famous stories of ghost ships is the *Flying Dutchman*, which sailed in 1680 from Amsterdam to Dutch East India under Hendrick Vanderdecken. When the captain ignored the danger warnings of a storm, his ship was smashed and the crew was lost. According to legend, his arrogance *invoked* the wrath of God, who condemned the lost crew-members to battle the waters off the Cape of Good Hope for eternity. Since then, there have been repeated sightings of the *Flying Dutchman*, one as recent as 1939. Many sightings of phantom ships occur in areas where vessels are known to have sunk. Sailors can never *divine* when or where they will next encounter a phantom ship. Rather, most of their sightings occur randomly, only later to bring forth information of a former sea *horror*. Some say that ghosts aboard a phantom ship are trying to use living sailors as their *intermediaries*. Still others think that the existence of phantom ships is merely a *self-perpetuating* myth for bored sailors who are prone to too much idle *meditation* about the meaning of life and death on the high seas.

1. How would the author explain phantom ships?

    a. Their appearance is tied to the stars.

    b. Sailors at sea have little to do.

    c. Fog and high waves can distort one's vision.

    d. Shipwreck remains haunt oceans around the world.

2. Why does the author mention the *Flying Dutchman?*

    a. as the basis of primitive navigation systems

    b. as an example of a commonly sighted phantom ship

    c. as the reason why many sailors have mental problems

    d. as an explanation for sightings of phantom ships

Lesson 13   Ghosts

    TOEFL Prep I   1. b   2. c   3. d   4. a   5. b

    TOEFL Prep II   1. psychic   2. haunting   3. phantoms   4. invoke

       5. divination

    TOEFL Success   1. b   2. b

ociety

Anthropology

Target Words

1. assimilate	6. relic
2. cremation	7. rite
3. domesticate	8. ritually
4. folklore	9. saga
5. fossilize	10. vestige

Definitions and Samples

1. **assimilate** *v.* To consume and incorporate; to become similar

   Not all of the overseas students could **assimilate** into the rigidly controlled school.

   Usage tips *Assimilate* is often followed by *into*.

   Parts of speech assimilation *n*

2. **cremation** *n.* The act of burning the dead

   Cremation is particularly common in Japan, where land for burial is very limited.

   Parts of speech cremate *v*

3. **domesticate** *v.* To make something suitable for being in a home

   The Barnes family hoped to **domesticate** the tiger, but their neighbors were skeptical.

Usage tips   The object of *domesticate* is usually a plant or animal.

Parts of speech   domestic *adj*

4. **folklore** *n.*   Traditional myths of a people transmitted orally

Through **folklore,** archaeologists have learned about the migration of Native Americans in North America.

Parts of speech   folkloric *adj*

5. **fossilize** *v.*   To become preserved in clay or stone or ash after death, so that a natural record is left of the original organism; to become rigid and stuck in old ways

The dinosaur eggs had **fossilized** over thousands of years.

Parts of speech   fossilization *n,* fossil *n*

6. **relic** *n.*   Something left from a long-ago culture, time period, or person

Relics of the war can still be found in the sand dunes along this shore.

7. **rite** *n.*   A ceremony meant to achieve a certain purpose

Many cultures have fertility **rites** that supposedly make it more likely for women to bear children.

8. **ritually** *adv.*   As part of a traditional ceremony or habit

The children **ritually** kissed their parents on the cheek before bed.

Parts of speech   ritual *n,* ritual *adj*

9. **saga** *n.*   A long story about important events long ago

Many American families tell **sagas** about their ancestors' arrival in the United States.

10. **vestige** *n.*   A visible trace that something once existed

The wilted flowers were the only **vestige** of their romantic weekend.

TOEFL Prep I Choose the word from the list that is closest in meaning to the underlined part of each sentence. Write it in the blank.

assimilate   cremation   domesticate   folklore   ritual

_____ 1. In many cultures around the world, young boys are circumcised in a <u>traditional</u> ceremony.

_____ 2. It is difficult to <u>tame</u> a bird that was born in the wild.

_____ 3. Based on the <u>oral legends</u> about the fire, researchers estimate that about half of the townspeople died in the blaze.

_____ 4. After the <u>burning of the body</u>, the remaining bits of bone are transferred to a large urn.

_____ 5. Her husband could never <u>fit into</u> her family's way of life.

TOEFL Prep II Write the best word next to each definition. Use each word only once.

fossilize   relic   rite   saga   vestige

_____ 1. to harden after death

_____ 2. a customary act

_____ 3. a memento

_____ 4. something remaining from the past

_____ 5. a long story

TOEFL Success Read the passage to review the vocabulary you have learned. Answer the questions that follow.

The aborigines of Australia may have been some of the first people on the planet. Recent discoveries of *relics,* including stone tools, show that humans lived near Penrith, New South Wales, about 47,000 years ago. Australian aborigines migrated from northern lands by sea, when the water passages were narrower than they are today. This is the first evidence of sea travel by prehistoric humans. The *saga* of this water passing survives in modern-day aboriginal *folklore*. To put this in perspective, remember that 50,000 years ago, humans were nomadic. Early aborigines did not cultivate crops, and in Australia at the time there were no animals that could be *domesticated*. No one knows how long it took aboriginal people to reach Australia, but archaeologists are searching through ancient campsites for *vestiges* of their early lifestyle. *Fossilized* remains indicate that these nomadic people not only gathered food from the land, but they also subsisted on meat from large animals that no longer exist today. As part of their hunting tradition, aborigines *ritually* covered themselves in mud to mask their own scent or for camouflage. Aboriginal society marked the major events of life with *rites* such as circumcision, marriage, and *cremation*. Older people were revered and cared for as great sources of wisdom. When Westerners arrived in Australia in 1788, the 300,000 aborigines who lived there were not eager to *assimilate* their ways. In the following years, disease, loss of land, and loss of identity shaped the aborigines' history perhaps as much as their first prehistoric crossing from the north.

> **Bonus Structure—** To put this in perspective *means "to give some background information."*

1. Which sentence best expresses the essential information in this passage?

   a. Australian aborigines were some of the Earth's first people.
   b. White explorers did not respect aboriginal culture.
   c. Australian aborigines probably migrated from Africa.
   d. The organization and functioning of aboriginal society is mostly unknown.

2. In this passage, the word *ritually* is closest in meaning to

   a. regularly
   b. ignorantly
   c. superstitiously
   d. dramatically

Lesson 14   Anthropology

TOEFL Prep I   1. ritual   2. domesticate   3. folklore
4. cremation   5. assimilate
TOEFL Prep II   1. fossilize   2. rite   3. relic   4. vestige   5. saga
TOEFL Success   1. a   2. a

Social Inequality

Target Words

1. amend	6. discriminate
2. biased	7. notion
3. burden	8. oppress
4. counter	9. paradigm
5. de facto	10. prejudiced

Definitions and Samples

1. amend *v.* To change for the better

The residents voted to **amend** their neighborhood policy on fences.

Parts of speech amendment *n*

2. biased *adj.* Leaning unfairly in one direction

Her newspaper article was criticized for being heavily **biased** toward the mayor's proposal.

Parts of speech bias *n*

3. burden *n.* Something that is carried; a source of stress or worry

The donkey walked slowly under the **burden** of its heavy load.

The failing company faced the **burden** of bad debts and a poor reputation.

Parts of speech burden *v*

4. **counter** *v.*   To act in opposition to; to offer in response

The hockey player **countered** the punch with a smashing blow from his hockey stick.

Jane **countered** every accusation with a specific example of her achievements.

Parts of speech   counter *n,* counter *adj*

5. **de facto** *adj.*   Truly doing a job, even if not officially

Popular support established the Citizens Party as the **de facto** government.

Parts of speech   de facto *adv*

6. **discriminate**   To choose carefully among options

The governor wisely **discriminated** between urgent issues and those that could wait.

Parts of speech   discriminatory *adj,* discriminate *adj*

7. **notion** *n.*   A belief; a fanciful impulse

The **notion** that older office equipment is unreliable is inaccurate.

One morning, she suddenly took the **notion** to paint her kitchen red.

Usage tips   *Notion* can be followed by a *that* clause or a *to* phrase.

8. **oppress** *v.*   To keep down by force; to weigh heavily on

Factory management **oppressed** workers through intimidation.

Parts of speech   oppression *n*

9. **paradigm** *n.*   A pattern or model; a set of assumptions

The usual **paradigm** for economic growth in developed countries does not apply to some poor nations.

Usage tips   *Paradigm* is often followed by *for.*

10. **prejudiced** *adj.*   Causing to judge prematurely and unfairly

Many consumers are **prejudiced** against commercial goods made in third-world countries.

Parts of speech   prejudice *v*, prejudice *n*

TOEFL Prep I   Complete each sentence by filling in the blank with the best word from the list. Change the form of the word if necessary. Use each word only once.

biased   counter   de facto   notion   paradigm

1. During the trial, the defense lawyer _____ each claim with an opposite charge.

2. The basketball coach was naturally _____ toward the taller players.

3. After we saw the fancy car that the Jacobses bought, we gave up the _____ that they could not afford the basic things in life.

4. The battle was successful, as judged by the prevailing _____ of that era.

5. Even though Jovie was a cleaner, not a nanny, she was the baby's _____ caregiver because his parents worked so many hours.

TOEFL Prep II   Find the word or phrase that is closest in meaning to the opposite of each word in the left-hand column. Write the letter in the blank.

_____ 1. amend   (a) relieve
_____ 2. burden   (b) allow to operate freely
_____ 3. oppress   (c) leave as is
_____ 4. indiscriminately   (d) unbiased
_____ 5. prejudiced   (e) by making careful choices

TOEFL Success   Read the passage to review the vocabulary you have learned. Answer the questions that follow.

Nelson Mandela devoted his life to fighting *prejudice* in South Africa. Mandela traveled his state, organizing a fight against *discriminatory* laws and racial *bias*. He encouraged civil disobedience as a tool against the *oppression* of Blacks. As deputy president of the African National Congress, Mandela encouraged his fellow citizens to challenge the prevailing *paradigm* of power. Mandela believed that prejudice *burdened* not only the oppressed, but also the oppressors.

The government *countered* Mandela's activities with a criminal conviction. Still, Mandela's *de facto* leadership gained him respect and authority among his fellow citizens. Mandela's courage and popularity worried **the ruling class,** who did not want to share power. What's more, they refused to <u>amend</u> the state's laws. So when Mandela returned from an overseas trip to gain support for his cause in 1962, he was arrested, jailed, and sentenced to life in prison for various crimes.

Bonus Structure— **The ruling class** *means those who held power mostly because of the families they were born into.*

This only fueled Mandela's *notions* about inequality and justice. He took his demands to jail, where he demanded the same dress and safety gear for Black prisoners as for White prisoners. After 28 years in prison, Mandela was released, returning immediately to public life. In 1994, he was elected the president of South Africa.

1. Which of the following best expresses the essential information of this passage?
   a. Nelson Mandela used illegal means to achieve his ends.
   b. Nelson Mandela fought prejudice in South Africa.
   c. Nelson Mandela inspired Blacks around the world.
   d. Nelson Mandela was driven primarily by his religious beliefs.

2. In the passage, the word <u>amend</u> is closest in meaning to
   a. ignore
   b. write down
   c. change
   d. discuss

Lesson 15   Social Inequality

TOEFL Prep I   1. countered   2. biased   3. notion   4. paradigm
5. de facto

TOEFL Prep II   1. c   2. a   3. b   4. e   5. d

TOEFL Success   1. b   2. c

Expertise

Target Words

1. curriculum	6. parochial
2. distinctly	7. rigor
3. erudite	8. roster
4. fortify	9. secular
5. implicitly	10. suspend

Definitions and Samples

1. **curriculum** *n.* The courses of study offered by an educational institution

   The teachers met to design a new **curriculum** for the Intensive English Program.

2. **distinctly** *adv.* Clearly

   I **distinctly** remember saying that we would meet at noon.

   Parts of speech distinction *n*, distinct *adj*

3. **erudite** *adj.* Highly educated

   Even though Stella was only a freshman, she was considered **erudite** by both her classmates and her professors.

4. **fortify** *v.* To strengthen

   The high-priced drink had extra vitamins and minerals to **fortify** the body.

   Parts of speech fortification *n*

5. **implicitly** *adv.*   Without being stated; unquestioningly

By joining the competition, she agreed **implicitly** to the rules.

Parts of speech   implicit *adj*

6. **parochial** *adj.*   Restricted in outlook; relating to the local parish

Marla moved from her rural community to get away from its **parochial** thinking.

Sending your children to a **parochial** school can cost as much as sending them to college.

7. **rigor** *n.*   Strictness; difficult situations that come from following rules strictly

The wrestler followed his diet with **rigor**.

The **rigors** of military life toughened the young men quickly.

Parts of speech   rigorous *adj*

8. **roster** *n.*   A list, especially of names

Two of the names on the **roster** were misspelled.

9. **secular** *adj.*   Worldly rather than spiritual; not related to religion

Few private schools in the United States are **secular**.

10. **suspend** *v.*   To cause to stop for a period; to hang as to allow free movement

The trial was **suspended** when the judge learned that one of the jury members knew the defense lawyer.

The circus acrobat was **suspended** in midair.

Parts of speech   suspension *n,* suspension *adj*

TOEFL Prep I   For each word, choose the word that has the most similar meaning. Write the letter of your choice on the line.

1. distinctly _____
   (a) clearly   (b) fully   (c) softly   (d) aggressively

2. erudite _____
   (a) strong   (b) wise   (c) complicated   (d) plain

3. fortify _____
   (a) weaken   (b) contemplate   (c) strengthen   (d) reshape

4. rigor _____
   (a) strictness   (b) talent   (c) peace   (d) recklessness

5. suspend _____
   (a) tie   (b) fill   (c) hang   (d) throw

TOEFL Prep II Choose the word from the list that is closest in meaning to the underlined part of each sentence. Write it in the blank.

curriculum   *implicitly*   *parochial*   *roster*   *secular*

_____ 1. The class <u>list</u> showed that only 12 students had enrolled for spring quarter.

_____ 2. Many parents feel that public schools are as good as <u>private, religious</u> schools.

_____ 3. The principal requested parents' feedback on the new <u>set of math classes</u>.

_____ 4. In the United States, many private grade schools are <u>not affiliated with a religion</u>.

_____ 5. The janitor agreed <u>indirectly</u> not to turn in the students.

TOEFL Success Read the passage to review the vocabulary you have learned. Answer the questions that follow.

In the last three decades, universities across the United States have attempted to adapt their *curriculums* to meet the changing purposes of higher education. University education was also once considered an exclusive opportunity, with *erudite* scholars establishing courses based on the goal of training a *distinctly* academic "elite." These days, not every undergraduate is destined to become a scholar, and the *roster* of students represents a more complete cross section of society, including minorities, women, and returning students. These days, most learners attend university to *fortify* basic skills, primarily learning how to learn and how to express themselves. Far from its earlier religious or <u>elitist</u> image, the university is seen increasingly as a *secular* center for career development, where students know they will graduate into a competitive job market. Most professors have embraced this evolution in the university's role,

> *Bonus Structure—* **On the other hand** *introduces an opposing point.*

letting go of the traditional, *parochial* view of higher education. **On the other hand,** many feel that while they want to accommodate an adaptable curriculum, universities must not *suspend* their obligation of establishing *rigorous* requirements for education and graduation. *Implicit* in their stance is support for the traditional liberal arts curriculum with a core of classes required across disciplines.

1. According to information in the reading, which of the following sentences would the author be most likely to agree with?

    a. Universities are becoming increasingly exclusive.
    b. A curriculum needs to be completely adaptable to students' needs.
    c. The role of higher education is changing, and so is the university curriculum.
    d. The cost of university puts it out of reach of many populations.

2. In this passage, the word <u>elitist</u> is closest in meaning to

    a. superior
    b. academic
    c. populist
    d. elegant

Lesson 16   Expertise

TOEFL Prep I   1. a   2. b   3. c   4. a   5. c
TOEFL Prep II   1. roster   2. parochial   3. curriculum   4. secular
     5. implicitly
TOEFL Success   1. c   2. a

Military Operations

Target Words

1. allegiance
2. artillery
3. battle
4. cease
5. hierarchy
6. in the trenches
7. mobilize
8. rank
9. ratio
10. strategic

Definitions and Samples

1. **allegiance** *n.* Loyalty

   My **allegiance** to my country is based on respect for its principles.

   Usage tips *Allegiance* is commonly followed by a *to* phrase.

2. **artillery** *n.* Large guns that shoot powerful shells; army units that handle such guns

   An **artillery** barrage broke down the city's thick walls within seconds. The 47th **Artillery** fired on rebels camped in the city center.

   Usage tips When it means a part of an army, *artillery* is sometimes plural.

3. **battle** *v.* To fight against

   The Viet Minh **battled** French forces at Dien Bien Phu for nearly two months in 1954.

   Parts of speech battle *n*

4. **cease** *v.*   Stop

The lightning continued even after the thunder had **ceased.**

Usage tips   *Cease* is found in official statements, not usually in everyday speech.

Parts of speech   cessation *n,* ceaseless *adj*

5. **hierarchy** *n.*   A system of levels that places people high or low according to their importance

Starting as a lowly private, Burt Jones gradually rose through the **hierarchy** of the army.

Usage tips   *Hierarchy* is often followed by an *of* phrase.

Parts of speech   hierarchical *adj,* hierarchically *adv*

6. **in the trenches** *adv'l.*   In the middle of the hardest fighting or work

With their unrealistic view of this war, our generals don't know what things are like out **in the trenches.**

Usage tips   Creates an image of soldiers fighting in a long, dug-out place in the battlefield.

7. **mobilize** *v.*   To put members of a group into motion

After a terrible storm, the governor **mobilized** the National Guard to rescue victims.

Parts of speech   mobilization *n*

8. **rank** *v.*   To put into a many-leveled order, depending on importance or achievement

The Marines **ranked** Jim Hurst highest among all their officer candidates.

Parts of speech   rank *n*

9. **ratio** *n.*   The relationship of one number or amount to another

Military analysts say that the **ratio** of attackers to defenders in a battle should be about three to one for the attackers to win.

Usage tips   *Ratio* is very often followed by an *of . . . to* structure.

10. **strategic** *adj.*   Related to long-term plans for achieving a goal

The United States has formed **strategic** friendships with Tajikistan and Mongolia to have Central Asian bases in the future.

Usage tips   *Strategic* is often used with nouns for plans.

Parts of speech   strategy *n,* strategize *v,* strategically *adv*

TOEFL Prep I   Find the word or phrase that is closest in meaning to the opposite of each word or phrase in the left-hand column. Write the letter in the blank.

_____ 1. cease	(a) stay still
_____ 2. artillery	(b) not in the fighting
_____ 3. mobilize	(c) continue
_____ 4. battle	(d) make peace
_____ 5. in the trenches	(e) light guns

TOEFL Prep II   Choose the word from the list that is closest in meaning to the underlined part of each sentence. Write it in the blank.

allegiance   *hierarchy*   *ranked*   *ratio*   *strategy*

_____ 1. Destruction of the enemy's radar defenses <u>was rated</u> very high in the plan of attack.

_____ 2. The president's constant mistakes weakened the army's <u>loyalty</u> to him.

_____ 3. Eventually, Gordon reached the highest level in the military's <u>system of positions</u>, that of five-star general.

_____ 4. The planet Mercury is so small that the <u>proportion</u> of its volume to Earth's is only about 1 to 20.

_____ 5. While other officers worried about day-to-day operations, General Helvetski kept his eye on <u>long-term plans</u>.

TOEFL Success   Read the passage to review the vocabulary you have learned. Answer the questions that follow.

Until a century ago, military medicine was poor at *battling* disease. The *ratio* of soldiers killed by diseases to those killed in combat was probably at least two to one. For *strategic* reasons, military camps were often set up near a body of water. This gave some protection from enemy *artillery,* but it exposed soldiers to disease-carrying mosquitoes. Mosquitoes also plagued troops *in the trenches.* Low-*ranking* troops suffered the most. Officers who were advanced enough in the *hierarchy* slept in separate tents on high ground.

> *Bonus Structure—*
> Until a century
> ago *indicates that*
> *the condition to*
> *be described*
> *stopped about*
> *100 years ago.*

The long-held belief that disease resulted from evil spirits or bad air eventually *ceased* to rule military medicine. The germ theory *mobilized* actual science against disease. General George Washington ordered that his men be vaccinated against smallpox. Their *allegiance* to him can be measured by the fact that they obeyed, for Washington's doctors used the actual smallpox virus, not the safer vaccination that Edward Jenner would introduce in 1798.

1. Which sentence best expresses the essential information of this passage?
   a. Army officers were far healthier than common foot soldiers.
   b. For a long time, a soldier was more likely to die of disease than in battle.
   c. Armies should camp on dry ground, not near water.
   d. Diseases are caused by viruses and spread by mosquitoes.

2. Why does the author mention that military camps were often set up near water?
   a. to explain why soldiers were not usually killed by artillery
   b. to show that officers and men did not mix
   c. to explain how soldiers came into contact with disease-carrying mosquitoes
   d. to show that water was valuable in treating "camp fever"

Lesson 17   Military Operations

    TOEFL Prep I   1. c   2. e   3. a   4. d   5. b

    TOEFL Prep II   1. ranked   2. allegiance   3. hierarchy   4. ratio
      5. strategy

    TOEFL Success   1. b   2. c

War and Conquest

Target Words

1. annex	6. invasive
2. apex	7. prevailing
3. collapse	8. resist
4. conquest	9. severely
5. devise	10. violation

Definitions and Samples

1. **annex** *v.*   To make something (usually land) part of another unit

   Bardstown grew by **annexing** several farms at the north edge of town.

   Parts of speech   annexation *n,* annex *n*

2. **apex** *n.*   The highest point

   Gregory knew that his running skills had to be at their **apex** during the tournament.

   Usage tips   *Apex* is often used to describe the high point of someone's abilities.

3. **collapse** *v.*   To fall down, usually because of weakness

   Parts of speech   collapse *n,* collapsible *adj*

4. **conquest** *n.*   A takeover by force or continued effort

The first recorded **conquest** of Mt. Everest was by Tensing Norgay and Sir Edmund Hilary.

Usage tips   *Conquest* is usually followed by an *of* phrase.

Parts of speech   conquer *v*

5. **devise** *v.*   To find an original way to make an object or a plan

The soldiers **devised** a way to cross the river into enemy territory without being seen.

Parts of speech   device *n*

6. **invasive** *adj.*   Aggressively entering into someone else's territory

Surgery with a laser is less **invasive** than surgery with a knife or scalpel.

Parts of speech   invade *v*, invasion *n*, invader *n*

7. **prevailing** *adj.*   Strongest or most common

The **prevailing** attitude among our neighbors is to be friendly but not too friendly.

Parts of speech   prevail *v*, prevalence *n*

8. **resist** *v.*   To refuse to give in to a strong force or desire

Although many native nations **resisted,** the U.S. government eventually took over almost all Indian land.

Parts of speech   resistance *n*, resistant *adj*

9. **severely** *adv.*   Harshly; extremely

Commanders **severely** punished any soldier who criticized the battle plan.

Parts of speech   severity *n*, severe *adj*

10. **violation** *n.*   An action that breaks a law or agreement; mistreatment of something that deserves respect

The army's testing of new weapons was a **violation** of the cease-fire agreement.

The sculptures at Mt. Rushmore may be a **violation** of sacred Indian land.

Usage tips   *Violation* is often followed by an *of* phrase.

Parts of speech   violate *v,* violator *n*

TOEFL Prep I   Find the word or phrase that is closest in meaning to each word in the left-hand column. Write the letter in the blank.

_____ 1. severely	(a) invent
_____ 2. prevailing	(b) fall down
_____ 3. devise	(c) add on
_____ 4. collapse	(d) extremely
_____ 5. annex	(e) most common

TOEFL Prep II   Circle the word that best completes each sentence.

1. The judge ruled that Harry was guilty of a (violation / conquest) of the seat-belt law.
2. Because Dalmatia was protected by high mountains, the empire could not (apex / annex) it.
3. We have to (conquest / devise) a way to fight this new disease.
4. Several armed groups joined together to (resist / collapse) the foreign invaders.
5. The (prevailing / invasive) belief held that the enemy's peace moves were not sincere.

TOEFL Success   Read the passage to review the vocabulary you have learned. Answer the questions that follow.

The Roman *conquest* of North Africa is, in the *prevailing* view, less interesting than Rome's European adventures. In truth, one of the first lands Rome *annexed* beyond the Italian peninsula was the area around Carthage in North Africa. Carthage and Rome had been in conflict (called the Punic Wars) since 264 BCE for control of trade along the Mediterranean coast. In 202 BCE, during the Second Punic War, the Carthaginian general Hannibal *devised* a clever plan, in *violation* of most military wisdom, to march through the high Alps to attack the Roman heartland. The cold weather and steep terrain *severely* stressed Hannibal's forces, many of whom rode elephants. The Romans *resisted* Hannibal's attacks, and his bold *invasion* force *collapsed.* **In the end,** Rome finished off Carthage in the Third Punic War (149–146 BCE). At its *apex* in 117 CE, Rome controlled all of North Africa and territories from the Persian Gulf to Britain.

> *Bonus Structure—* **In the end** *introduces the last stage of a long process.*

1. Which sentence best expresses the essential information of this passage?

   a. Romans were very successful at resisting invaders.
   b. Hannibal tried crossing the Alps on elephants to invade Rome.
   c. Rome and Carthage fought three wars, known as the Punic Wars.
   d. One of Rome's first overseas conquests was of the North African state of Carthage.

2. The author of this passage believes that Hannibal's attack on Rome by crossing the Alps was _____.

   a. not what most military commanders would do
   b. exactly what the Roman army used to do
   c. cruel to elephants
   d. impractical because elephants can't cross mountains

Lesson 18 War and Conquest

TOEFL Prep I 1. d 2. e 3. a 4. b 5. c
TOEFL Prep II 1. violation 2. annex 3. devise 4. resist
   5. prevailing
TOEFL Success 1. d 2. a

History

Target Words

1. chronologically
2. coincide
3. consequence
4. core
5. deny
6. diminish
7. longitude
8. milieu
9. Orwellian
10. reconciliation

Definitions and Samples

1. **chronologically** *adv.* In order according to time

    Allen's book is arranged **chronologically,** from the First Crusade in 1095 to the fall of Granada in 1492.

    Usage tips *Chronologically* is often used with *arranged, organized, listed,* or some other word for order.

    Parts of speech chronology *n*, chronological *adj*

2. **coincide** *v.* Happen or exist at the same time

    The Viking attacks on western Europe **coincided** with an abnormally warm period in the Earth's climate.

    Usage tips *Coincide* is often followed by a *with* phrase.

    Parts of speech coincidence *n*, coincidental *adj*, coincidentally *adv*

3. **consequence** *n.* A result, often one much later in time than the cause

    One **consequence** of global warming may be the flooding of low-lying islands.

Usage tips *Consequence* usually implies something negative or serious about the result.

Parts of speech consequent *adj*, consequently *adv*

4. **core** *n.* an area or object at the center

The **core** of India's film industry is in Bombay, where all but a few film studios are located.

Usage tips *Core* is often followed by another noun (e.g., *core principle*) or by an *of* phrase.

5. **deny** *v.* Say that something is not true

Movie star Allen Butcher **denied** that he and the Princess of Denmark were getting married.

Usage tips *Deny* is often followed by the *-ing* form of a verb or by a *that* clause.

Parts of speech denial *n*, deniably *adv*

6. **diminish** *v.* Make something smaller or weaker; become smaller or weaker

The Protestant Reformation **diminished** the power of the Roman Catholic Pope.

Mr. Partridge's influence in the company **diminished** after he relocated to a branch office.

7. **longitude** *n.* A system of imaginary lines running from north to south along the Earth's surface, where each line is numbered from 0° to 180° west or east

The prime meridian, a line running through Greenwich, England, is marked as 0° **longitude.**

Parts of speech longitudinal *adj*, longitudinally *adv*

8. **milieu** *n.* General environment or surroundings

Many Vietnam veterans did not feel comfortable in the antiwar social **milieu** of the 1970s.

9. **Orwellian** *adj.*   Frightening and overcontrolled by a government that interferes in nearly every aspect of personal life

Biometric devices like eye-scanners allow an **Orwellian** level of government knowledge about everyone's location.

10. **reconciliation** *n.*   Coming back together peacefully after having been enemies

South Africa avoided a bloodbath after apartheid by setting up a Truth and **Reconciliation** Commission.

Parts of speech   reconcile *v,* reconciliatory *adj*

TOEFL Prep I   Find the word or phrase that is closest in meaning to each word in the left-hand column. Write the letter in the blank.

_____ 1. deny	(a) say something isn't true
_____ 2. chronologically	(b) an end to being enemies
_____ 3. consequence	(c) middle
_____ 4. reconciliation	(d) in the order in which events happened
_____ 5. core	(e) result

TOEFL Prep II   Circle the word that best completes each sentence.

1. When a nation becomes unwilling to listen to its allies, its international influence will (deny / diminish).
2. The release of many new movies (coincides / consequences) with the start of the holiday period.
3. The (core / milieu) of Roman power shifted to Constantinople after Rome was attacked repeatedly by armies from the north.
4. As our government becomes better at monitoring us, an (Orwellian / coincidental) future awaits us.
5. As you move directly east from one point on the Earth to another, your (longitude / chronology) changes.

TOEFL Success Read the passage to review the vocabulary you have learned. Answer the questions that follow.

Revisionist history promotes a new view of *chronological* events, usually for political purposes. Radical revisionists *diminish* the credibility of a previous view and may even *deny* that certain events happened at all. Some revisionist Asian historians have ignored long-standing conflicts among native peoples and have explained Asia's conflicts as a *consequence* of colonialism and its class-oriented cultural *milieu*. **Good motives** among the revisionists—to promote *reconciliation* among traditional rivals—**don't excuse bad history**. History is valuable only if its stories *coincide* with verifiable facts. From far away, an observer may see clearly that a given conflict had nothing to do with colonialism and a lot to do with 1,000-year-old rivalries. But this is not likely to matter much to a confirmed revisionist historian. At its *core*, revisionism—by the government in particular—is an *Orwellian* exercise in thought control, not honest science.

> **Bonus Structure—Good motives don't excuse bad history.** *Even though revisionists are trying to achieve a good social goal, they shouldn't distort history to do so.*

1. Which sentence best expresses the essential information of this passage?

   a. Historians constantly revise history in the light of new facts.
   b. Revisionist history is less concerned with accuracy than with promoting a point of view.
   c. A new way of studying history, revisionism, has been very successful in Asia.
   d. Revisionist history is the only way to accurately relate events.

2. Why does the author of this reading mention Asia?

   a. because it offers an example of attempts at revisionist history
   b. because a civil war occurred between revisionists and others
   c. because it is the birthplace of revisionist history
   d. because it was colonized by Europeans and needs a revisionist history

Lesson 19 History

TOEFL Prep I   1. a   2. d   3. e   4. b   5. c

TOEFL Prep II   1. diminish   2. coincides   3. core   4. Orwellian
5. longitude

TOEFL Success   1. b   2. a

Money

Financial Systems

Target Words

1. allocate	6. net
2. commodity	7. per capita
3. decline	8. regulate
4. equity	9. subsidy
5. inflation	10. tangible

Definitions and Samples

1. **allocate** *v.* To give out different amounts for different purposes

   The budget **allocates** $58 billion to the military and only about $2 billion to education.

   Usage tips Things that can be *allocated* are things that can be "spent"—money, time, energy, etc.

   Parts of speech allocation *n*

2. **commodity** *n.* A thing that can be bought and sold, such as grain, oil, or wood

   Tulip bulbs were one of the most valuable **commodities** in seventeenth-century Holland.

   Usage tips A thing is called a *commodity* only in the context of buying or selling it.

3. **decline** *v.*   To decrease in power or amount

America's railroads **declined** because the automobile dominated American life.

Parts of speech   decline *n*

4. **equity** *n.*   The value of one's share in an investment

Barnard's **equity** in the business was one-third, or about $350,000.

Usage tips   In this meaning, *equity* is always singular and usually followed by an *in* phrase.

5. **inflation** *n.*   A situation in which prices for many items rise quite fast

During the rapid **inflation** of the 1970s, prices for food and fuel sometimes rose 20 percent in a single month.

Parts of speech   inflate *v*, inflationary *adj*

6. **net** *adj.*   After all costs have been subtracted from an amount

My gross salary is around $35,000, but my **net** pay is closer to $29,000.

Parts of speech   net *v*, net *n*

7. **per capita** *adv.*   For each person

Research shows we're likely to sell 15 light bulbs **per capita** per year in medium-sized cities.

Parts of speech   per capita *adj*

8. **regulate** *v.*   Control according to a set of rules

Trading on the New York Stock Exchange is **regulated** by officials of the exchange and by federal law.

Parts of speech   regulation *n*, regulatory *adj*

9. **subsidy** *n.*   Money given by a government or other organization to support an activity

Federal **subsidies** to grain farmers have helped them stay in business despite three years of bad weather.

Parts of speech   subsidize *v*

10. **tangible** *adj.* Obviously real because it can be seen, touched, or otherwise observed

One **tangible** benefit of putting electrical cables underground is a clearer view of the sky.

TOEFL Prep I Cross out the one word or phrase that doesn't fit into each of the lists.

1. things that can be allocated
        money   time   temperature   attention
2. kinds of commodities
        oil   sadness   corn   meat
3. tangible things
        fairness   a road   trees   money
4. things you can have equity in
        a company   a house   a child   a racehorse

TOEFL Prep II Circle the word that best completes each sentence.

1. Buy a car now, before (equity / inflation) drives the price up.
2. Most investors make a mistake. During a stock-market (decline / subsidy) they get frightened and sell.
3. The government is giving a (regulation / subsidy) to tobacco farmers so they can compete with foreign producers.
4. Cortecal Inc. estimates that it spends $80.00 (per capita / net) on its annual picnic and on its New Year party for the company's 1,300 employees.
5. I think that artificial "holidays" like Valentine's Day or Secretary's Day are just an attempt to turn private feelings into a(n) (commodity / equity).

TOEFL Success Read the passage to review the vocabulary you have learned. Answer the questions that follow.

The great unsettled question of economics is: "How much should the government *regulate* business?" Conservatives generally argue for a *decline* in government involvement, but they favor certain *subsidies* to farmers, steelmakers, or airplane manufacturers. Some conservatives also see no conflict between their small-government views and their eagerness for the government to *allocate* more money for roads into national forests. The *net* result of these incursions into national forests is a *tangible* infrastructure that helps some companies but not the public. Publicly owned trees, land, and oil become *commodities* from which a few private companies (many owned by small-government conservatives) profit. No *per capita* benefit goes to the American people, **aside perhaps from** the brief anti-*inflation* effect that comes with new oil exploration.

Bonus Structure—
Aside perhaps
from *means*
"maybe except for."

1. What is the main idea of this reading?

   a. Conservatives have tried to keep others from expanding government regulations.

   b. Even though conservatives say they want to limit government involvement in business, they actually do often favor it.

   c. There are several views about the proper role for government in business.

   d. Small-government conservatives want the government to allocate a certain amount of federal money per capita to help all Americans.

2. Which of the following does the author claim?

   a. Industries will become subsidies.

   b. Oil exploration causes inflation.

   c. Some elements of nature will become commodities.

   d. Infrastructure will be made of trees, oil, and land.

Lesson 20 Financial Systems

TOEFL Prep I 1. temperature   2. sadness   3. fairness   4. a child

TOEFL Prep II 1. inflation   2. decline   3. subsidy   4. per capita
    5. commodity

TOEFL Success 1. b   2. c

Wealth and Social Class

Target Words

1. accumulate	6. nobility
2. affluence	7. prestige
3. elite	8. privileged
4. impoverish	9. prosper
5. luxury	10. working class

Definitions and Samples

1. **accumulate** *v.*   To build up a large amount of something

   Over several generations, the Hardington family **accumulated** vast wealth by buying and selling land.

   Parts of speech   accumulation *n*

2. **affluence** *n.*   Wealth and the style of life that goes with it

   Mohadzir grew up amid **affluence,** which poorly prepared him for his grad student days in crowded apartments with no servants.

   Parts of speech   affluent *adj*

3. **elite** *adj.*   Belonging to a special, honored group

   Messner is an **elite** climber who recently ascended an 8,000-meter mountain without extra oxygen.

   Parts of speech   elite *n*, elitist *adj*

4. **impoverish** *v.*   To make a person or group poor

The collapse of the steel industry **impoverished** several counties in eastern Ohio.

Parts of speech   impoverishment *n*

5. **luxury** *n.*   Extreme comfort, beyond what anyone needs

Automakers try to give their cars an image of **luxury** by including extras like heated seats and satellite tracking systems.

Parts of speech   luxuriate *v*, luxurious *adj*

6. **nobility** *n.*   A group of socially prominent people with special titles given by a king or queen, such as "duke" or "countess"

In the Middle Ages, the **nobility** supposedly followed a code that required them to take care of poorer people who lived near their estates.

Usage tips   *Nobility* is used as a name for a group of distinguished people; it can also mean "a highly dignified form of behavior."

Parts of speech   noble *n*, noble *adj*

7. **prestige** *n.*   Honor and respect for being better than the average

The Grassleys enjoyed the **prestige** of living in the historic town, but they did not feel at home there.

Parts of speech   prestigious *adj*

8. **privileged** *adj.*   Able to enjoy special advantages because of one's position (usually because of being born into a wealthy or powerful family)

Despite his **privileged** position in one of America's most powerful families, the politician tried to portray himself as an ordinary person.

Parts of speech   privilege *n*

9. **prosper** *v.*   To do very well in one's business or personal life

Vargas **prospered** after finally patenting his new inventions.

Usage tips   A person can prosper; so can a group, a company, or an area.

Parts of speech   prosperity *n,* prosperous *adj*

10. **working class** *n.*   People with low-paying (often unskilled) jobs who are not poor but who are not securely in the middle class

    The Farrelly family, like other members of the **working class,** were proud of their jobs and did not want any handouts from charity or the government.

TOEFL Prep I   Find the word or phrase that is closest in meaning to each word in the left-hand column. Write the letter in the blank. Note: Many words in this chapter are similar in meaning. Pay careful attention to small differences in meaning.

_____ 1. impoverish		(a) enjoying special advantages
_____ 2. elite		(b) to succeed
_____ 3. prosper		(c) to make extremely poor
_____ 4. accumulate		(d) belonging to a small group with excellent achievements
_____ 5. privileged		(e) build up wealth

TOEFL Prep II   Complete each sentence by filling in the blank with the best word or phrase from the list. Change the form of the word if necessary. Use each word only once.

affluence   luxury   nobility   prestige   working class

1. The _____ in the hotel was obvious from such features as solid-gold faucets and stairs made of Italian marble.

2. In a show of his extreme _____, Jim Lavich flew 1,500 people to the Bahamas for his wife's birthday party and ordered 300 casks of wine for them to drink.

3. The oldest and most respected furniture maker in western Michigan, VanEden Inc., earned its _____ by using good materials and listening to its customers.

4. France's _____ was dismantled after the royal family was killed and lesser aristocrats were jailed during the revolution.

5. In the United States, many _____ families do not have health insurance because their employers don't offer it.

TOEFL Success   Read the passage to review the vocabulary you have learned. Answer the questions that follow.

The United States is not the land of equal opportunity. There are no titles of *nobility* as in Europe, but astounding *affluence* is passed on in *privileged* families, and this makes all the difference. **Studies in the 1970s** found that a child of the *elite* and a child of the *working class* may start out with similar intelligence and drive, but the rich child is about 30 times more likely to *prosper*. The rich child goes to high-*prestige* schools, where his or her education may be only slightly above average, but where the child *accumulates* friendships with future leaders.

> *Bonus Structure—The reference to studies in the 1970s indicates some objective evidence for the author's point.*

The privileged child becomes comfortable with *luxury* and is at ease in situations where powerful people meet. The working-class child from a less-prestigious college is not likely to wind up *impoverished*, but neither is he or she likely to attend many parties of Yale or Vassar alumni.

1. Which sentence best expresses the essential information of this passage?

   a. The American economy is unfair and must be changed.
   b. Rich people have natural advantages in education and social contacts that help them succeed.
   c. Children accept one another as friends; only later in life do differences of wealth drive them apart.
   d. The only way to make money in America is to work and accumulate it yourself.

2. Why does the author of this reading mention Yale and Vassar?

   a. They are elite schools attended by many future leaders.
   b. They are where government officials have secret meetings.

c. They try to give working-class children a chance they can't get at other schools.

d. Their high fees impoverish working-class children.

Lesson 21   Wealth and Social Class

TOEFL Prep I   1. c   2. d   3. b   4. e   5. a

TOEFL Prep II   1. luxury   2. affluence   3. prestige   4. nobility
   5. working class

TOEFL Success   1. b   2. a

Personal Property

Target Words

1. acquire	6. lease
2. assess	7. liability
3. asset	8. proprietor
4. hazardous	9. safeguard
5. jointly	10. sole

Definitions and Samples

1. **acquire** *v.* To get something, usually something with special value or meaning

   Bart hoped to **acquire** the 1898 D Indian Head penny, which would make his collection complete.

   Usage tips Unlike *get*, *acquire* implies that a possession has special value or meaning.

   Parts of speech acquisition *n,* acquisitive *adj*

2. **assess** *v.* To estimate the value of something

   The Barnes building was **assessed** at $1.3 million, but it can probably sell for much more than that.

   Parts of speech assessor *n,* assessment *n*

3. **asset** *n.* A possession that has positive value

   Usage tips Some examples of assets are real estate, cash, and stock shares.

4. **hazardous** *adj.*   Dangerous

Parents have to be careful not to buy children's clothes and toys made of **hazardous** materials.

Parts of speech   hazard *n,* hazardously *adv*

5. **jointly** *adv.*   Together with one or more other parties

In most states, a husband and wife are assumed to own all their possessions **jointly.**

Parts of speech   join *v,* joint *n*

6. **lease** *v.*   To rent something for a long time (several months or years)

Some drivers prefer to **lease** a car rather than buy one.

Parts of speech   lease *n,* lessor *n,* lessee *n*

7. **liability** *n.*   Legal responsibility for harming a person or property; a disadvantage

Before you go river rafting, you sign a document releasing the trip leaders from **liability** in case of injury.

Henderson is just a **liability** to our work team, because he never finishes anything on time.

Usage tips   In its second meaning, *liability* is often followed by a *to* phrase.

Parts of speech   liable *adj*

8. **proprietor** *n.*   Owner, usually of a business or a building

The **proprietor** of Hekman's Windows is Nels Hekman, grandson of the people who established the factory.

Usage tips   Very often, *proprietor* is followed by an *of* phrase.

Parts of speech   proprietary *adj*

9. **safeguard** *v.*   To protect

A burglar-alarm system **safeguards** our house when we go away on vacation.

Usage tips   *Safeguard* implies continuous protection over a long time.

10. sole *adj.*   Only

> Many people have wanted to invest in Harry's publishing business, but he remains the **sole** owner.

Usage tips *Sole* almost always appears before the noun it modifies. It does not come after a linking verb like *be.*

Parts of speech solely *adv*

TOEFL Prep I   Find the word that is closest in meaning to each word in the left-hand column. Write the letter in the blank.

_____ 1. assess	(a) dangerous
_____ 2. hazardous	(b) evaluate
_____ 3. jointly	(c) protect
_____ 4. liability	(d) responsibility
_____ 5. safeguard	(e) together

TOEFL Prep II   Circle the word that best completes each sentence.

1. The building company is trying to (safeguard / acquire) the whole neighborhood so it can put up a mall.
2. To the average farm family, every child was (an asset / a liability), one more set of hands to gather eggs or plant beans.
3. Gary's Cookie Shop has to move because the owner of the building won't renew the (lease / asset).
4. The (hazardous / sole) adult influence on Sarah as she grew up was her grandmother.
5. Some people are born with the disease, but others (acquire / assess) it later in life.

TOEFL Success   Read the passage to review the vocabulary you have learned. Answer the questions that follow.

It is not easy to make a living as the *proprietor* of apartment buildings. There is a huge initial expense, not only to *acquire* the properties but to *assess* the buildings and to remove any *hazardous* materials like lead-based paint. A landlord also has to buy the best *liability* insurance available just to *safeguard* the investment. Otherwise, one tragic accident could wipe out the value of the entire *asset.* Because of this expense, **it's rare** to find a *sole* individual owning such a property. The risk is more often taken on *jointly* by a group of investors who then split the profits from the *leases.*

> *Bonus Structure—* **It's rare** *is the opposite of "it's common."*

1. What is the main idea of this reading?

   a. Being a landlord is enjoyable.
   b. It costs a lot of money to be a landlord.
   c. Friendships can be destroyed by owning property jointly.
   d. Income from leases is greater than a landlord's expenses.

2. Which of the following is *not* an expense mentioned in the reading?

   a. property taxes
   b. insurance
   c. making the property safe
   d. buying the building you hope to rent

Lesson 22   Personal Property

TOEFL Prep I   1. b   2. a   3. e   4. d   5. c
TOEFL Prep II   1. acquire   2. asset   3. lease   4. sole   5. acquire
TOEFL Success   1. b   2. a

Employment

Target Words

1. compensate	6. **industrious**
2. dynamic	7. **marginal**
3. enterprising	8. **merit**
4. exploit	9. **promote**
5. incentive	10. **resign**

Definitions and Samples

1. **compensate** *v.* To give an employee money or other things in exchange for the work he or she does

   My pay doesn't properly **compensate** me for my efforts, but my other benefits, like health insurance, fill in the gap.

   Usage tips *Compensate* is often followed by a *for* phrase.

   Parts of speech compensation *n*, compensatory *adj*

2. **dynamic** *adj.* Full of energy

   This job requires a **dynamic** person, someone who will look for opportunities instead of just waiting around for them.

   Parts of speech dynamism *n*, dynamically *adv*

3. **enterprising** *adj.*   Creative in thinking of ways to make money

Immigrants are often among the most **enterprising** members of society, partly because anyone brave enough to make an overseas move is likely to be a risk-taker.

Parts of speech   enterprise *n* (Note: There is no verb "to enterprise.")

4. **exploit** *v.*   To take advantage of; to treat inconsiderately in order to profit

The company tried to **exploit** the low interest rates to expand operations.

The foreign mining company **exploited** our copper resources and then simply left.

Parts of speech   exploitation *n,* exploitive *adj*

5. **incentive** *n.*   A possible benefit that motivates a person to do a certain thing

This city's willingness to support its public schools gave us an **incentive** to move here with our two young children.

Usage tips   *Incentive* is usually followed by a *to* phrase.

6. **industrious** *adj.*   Willing to work hard

The Dutch settlements in Ottawa County were founded by **industrious** farmers who objected to frivolous behavior such as dancing.

Usage tips   Only people can be *industrious;* companies cannot.

Parts of speech   industriousness *n,* industriously *adv*

7. **marginal** *adj.*   Not very significant or effective

Our new advertising campaign had only **marginal** success, raising sales by a mere 3 percent.

Parts of speech   marginally *adv*

8. **merit** *n.*   Value; success based on one's work, not on luck

Pay raises at our company are based on **merit,** as determined by a committee of managers.

Usage tips *Merit* is uncountable.

Parts of speech merit *v*, meritorious *adj*

9. **promote** *v.* To move someone to a higher position in a company

  Because of his excellent handling of the Vredeman account, Jim Harris was **promoted** to vice president.

Usage tips *Promote* is very often followed by a *to* phrase indicating the position one has been moved up to.

Parts of speech promotion *n*

10. **resign** *v.* To quit one's job

  Because of controversy over his leadership style, Morton **resigned** from his job as president.

Parts of speech resignation *n*

TOEFL Prep I Find the word or phrase that is closest in meaning to each word in the left-hand column. Write the letter in the blank.

_____ 1. compensate	(a) good at finding business opportunities
_____ 2. dynamic	(b) hard-working
_____ 3. enterprising	(c) energetic
_____ 4. industrious	(d) move up
_____ 5. promote	(e) pay

TOEFL Prep II Circle the word that best completes each sentence.

1. Some companies move their factories to poor countries in order to (exploit / compensate) the desperation of people who are willing to work for very low wages.
2. For the last five years, we've seen only (dynamic / marginal) improvements in our productivity.
3. Judging by actual money-generating (promotion / merit), Williams is the company's most valuable employee.

4. I had a lot of (compensation / incentive) to move to our new facility in Minnesota, because two of my brothers live there.

5. Unless my employer stops polluting local rivers, I'm going to (resign / exploit).

TOEFL Success   Read the passage to review the vocabulary you have learned. Answer the questions that follow.

In the 1960s and 1970s, America was reaching the end of its role as a manufacturing power. Old-style systems of *compensation,* **especially** company pension plans, were impoverishing many companies. Much to the disadvantage of less-*industrious* workers, companies started demanding *merit,* not just seniority, before someone could be *promoted.* Many managers who were only *marginally* effective were encouraged to *resign.* These changes were painful, but

> *Bonus Structure—*
> **Especially**
> *introduces an outstanding example.*

unavoidable, symptoms of a growth spurt in the U.S. economy. Economies grow and change just as people do. A truly *enterprising* businessperson knows how to *exploit* these large changes and become involved in tomorrow's *dynamic* businesses, not yesterday's. There's still plenty of money to be made in America, a very effective *incentive* for workers to adapt to new conditions.

1. Which sentence best expresses the essential information of this passage?

   a. Most companies cannot afford to compensate their employees like they used to.

   b. Anyone interested in making a lot of money should move to the United States.

   c. The 1960s and 1970s were times of great change for the American economy.

   d. Just as retailers adapt to economic change, so must manufacturers.

2. The author of this article expresses a negative opinion about

   _____.

   a. businesspersons

   b. workers who depended on seniority for promotion

    c. companies that exploit changes in the economy
    d. the American economy as a whole

Lesson 23   Employment

TOEFL Prep I 1. e 2. c 3. a 4. b 5. d
TOEFL Prep II 1. exploit 2. marginal 3. merit 4. incentive
    5. resign
TOEFL Success 1. c 2. b

International Trade

Target Words

1. distill	6. merchant
2. entrepreneurial	7. proportionately
3. extract	8. prototype
4. haggle	9. reward
5. intrepid	10. shuttle

Definitions and Samples

1. **distill** *v.* to remove one liquid from a mixture of liquids by boiling; to get something valuable from a confusing mix of ideas

   The forest peoples of Southeast Asia **distill** an alcoholic drink called *arak* from a paste of palm berries.

   Most students are confused by her lectures, but Joe can always **distill** her main idea.

   Parts of speech distillation *n*, distillery *n*

2. **entrepreneurial** *adj.* Able to create business opportunities from a wide variety of circumstances

   Many engineers of the 1970s made great computers, but only a few were **entrepreneurial** enough to see the business possibilities in the new machines.

   Parts of speech entrepreneur *n*

3. **extract** *v.*   To take out

International mining companies came to the Malay Peninsula to **extract** the region's massive tin deposits.

Parts of speech   extraction *n,* extractor *n*

4. **haggle** *v.*   To argue back and forth about a price

The customer and the shopkeeper **haggled** over the silver plate for more than an hour.

Usage tips   *Haggle* is often followed by a phrase with *over* or *about.*

Parts of speech   haggler *n*

5. **intrepid** *adj.*   Fearless

For nearly 200 years, only the most **intrepid** colonists would cross the Appalachian Mountains.

6. **merchant** *n.*   A person who makes a living by selling things

The spice **merchants** of the eastern markets charged top prices to the Dutch and British sailors, who had come too far to sail away without buying.

Usage tips   The word *merchant* might be preceded by another noun telling what the merchant sells (e.g., *spice merchant* or *wine merchant*).

Parts of speech   merchandise *v,* merchandise *n,* mercantile *adj*

7. **proportionately** *adv.*   In an amount appropriate to each of several recipients

The food aid was distributed **proportionately** per family, with larger families receiving more.

Parts of speech   proportion *n,* proportionate *adj,* proportionally *adv*

8. **prototype** *n.*   The first one made of a machine or system

The airplane manufacturer uses robots to test every **prototype,** just in case there is a problem with the design.

9. **reward** *n.*   Something one gets for having done well

The greatest **reward** of being a parent is to see your child make a wise decision.

Usage tips   Reward might be followed by an *of* or *for* phrase naming what one has done well.

Parts of speech   reward *v*

10. **shuttle** *v.*   To move back and forth often between two places

The small jet **shuttles** between Kuala Lumpur and Singapore nearly every two hours.

Parts of speech   shuttle *n*

TOEFL Prep I   Find the word or phrase that is closest in meaning to each word in the left-hand column. Write the letter in the blank.

_____ 1. haggle   (a) brave
_____ 2. intrepid   (b) in appropriate amounts
_____ 3. extract   (c) argue about price
_____ 4. entrepreneurial (d) take out
_____ 5. proportionately (e) business-oriented

TOEFL Prep II   Circle the word that best completes each sentence.

1. To avoid disease, many people drink only (distilled / extracted) water, which has been boiled to evaporation and then recondensed on a cold surface.
2. Most business travelers do not find it exciting to (haggle / shuttle) between one location and another.
3. According to the laws in this state, tobacco can be sold only by certain licensed (merchants / entrepreneurs) at special tobacco stores.
4. One early (reward / prototype) of the computer was called ENIAC and was as big as an average-sized laboratory.
5. The children were punished (intrepidly / proportionately), with the leader getting a longer sentence than the followers.

TOEFL Success   Read the passage to review the vocabulary you have learned. Answer the questions that follow.

Tomatoes, potatoes, and hot peppers, all originally from South or Central America, are among several plants that have *disproportionately* influenced cooking around the world. This happened only after a few *intrepid* eaters got beyond common fears about potatoes, tomatoes, and other products. *Entrepreneurial* hunters for new food products hardly knew what they were *haggling* for when they tried to *extract* from foreign markets goods that would sell well at home. *Shuttling* between Europe and exotic lands, Italians, Spaniards, and Britons in particular brought back food *prototypes* that were not obviously good things to eat — cinnamon bark, cousins of the dreaded nightshade (tomatoes), and even the pollen from a crocus flower (saffron). As a glance at international cookbooks will show, many creative *merchants* were well *rewarded* not just with financial success, but with culture-changing influence.

Bonus Structure— **As a glance at** *introduces evidence for the author's claim.*

1. According to this reading, why did merchants have "culture-changing influence"?

    a. They found new ways to get from one country to another.
    b. Many of the plants they sold were poisonous and killed off some populations.
    c. They made it possible for cultures to develop new dishes.
    d. They spread European cooking habits around the world.

2. Cinnamon, tomatoes, and saffron are mentioned to make the point that

    _____ .

    a. many of the new plants merchants introduced were from Asia
    b. some strange-looking foods from odd sources were eventually accepted
    c. nightshade was unfairly dreaded by Europeans
    d. nearly every part of a plant can be turned into a kind of food

Lesson 24   International Trade

TOEFL Prep I   1. c   2. a   3. d   4. e   5. b
TOEFL Prep II   1. distilled   2. shuttle   3. merchants
   4. prototype   5. proportionately
TOEFL Success   1. c   2. b

Government
and Justice

Politics

Target Words

1. advocate
2. authority
3. bitterly
4. candidate
5. coalition

6. contest
7. election
8. inaugurate
9. policy
10. poll

Definitions and Samples

1. **advocate** *v.*   To speak out in favor of something

    Some environmentalists **advocate** removing large dams from the Columbia River.

    Usage tips   *Advocate* is usually followed by a term for a process or action, very often the *-ing* form of a verb

    Parts of speech   advocate *n,* advocacy *n*

2. **authority** *n.*   The power to make decisions, to tell others what to do.

    The governor has the **authority** to call the legislature together for emergency sessions.

    Usage tips   A *to* phrase often follows *authority.*

    Parts of speech   authorize *v,* authoritative *adj*

3. **bitterly** *adv.*   Strongly and with a lot of bad feelings

Senator Thomas **bitterly** opposed the movement to design a new state flag.

Parts of speech   bitterness *n,* bitter *adj*

4. **candidate** *n.*   Someone who wants to be chosen, especially in an election, for a position

In most U.S. elections, there are only two major-party **candidates** for president.

Usage tips   *Candidate* is often followed by a *for* phrase.

Parts of speech   candidacy *n*

5. **coalition** *n.*   A group of several different groups or countries that are working together to achieve a certain goal.

Several local churches, mosques, synagogues, and temples formed a **coalition** to promote understanding among people of different religions.

6. **contest** *v.*   To challenge

Dave Roper, who narrowly lost the mayor's race, **contested** the results, demanding a recount of the votes.

Usage tips   The noun *contest* can mean a game, especially one played for a prize.

Parts of speech   contest *n*

7. **election** *n.*   A process in which people choose officials

Because of problems with vote-counting four years ago, international observers monitored this year's **election** to make sure it was fair.

Parts of speech   elect *v,* elective *adj*

8. **inaugurate** *v.*   To bring into public office; to start formally

The U.S. president is elected in November but is not **inaugurated** until the following January.

An effort to bring electric service to farms and small towns was **inaugurated** with the Rural Electrification Act of 1936.

Usage tips When it means "bring into public office," *inaugurate* is usually in the passive voice.

Parts of speech inauguration *n*, inaugural *adj*

9. **policy** *n.* An approved way for approaching a certain kind of situation

The **policy** said that government money could not be given to any private hospital.

10. **poll** *v.* To find out a small group's opinion so that you can guess what a much larger group thinks

The newspaper **polled** 500 registered voters and found that only 27 percent were in favor of expanding the city zoo.

Parts of speech poll *n*, pollster *n*

TOEFL Prep I Find the phrase that best describes each word in the left-hand column. Write the letter in the blank.

_____ 1. policy   (a) a process of choosing
_____ 2. candidate   (b) a kind of power
_____ 3. authority   (c) a kind of person
_____ 4. coalition   (d) a way of handling a situation
_____ 5. election   (e) a kind of group

TOEFL Prep II Complete each sentence by filling in each blank with the best word from the list. Change the form of the word if necessary. Use each word only once.

advocated   *bitterly*   *contest*   *inaugurated*   *polled*

1. In the early twentieth century, politicians fought _____ about whether the U.S. dollar should be based on gold.

2. Only one month after he was _____, President Harrison fell sick and died.

3. My opponent says that I cheated on my taxes. I _____ that charge, and I will prove him wrong.

4. Their predictions about the election results were not very accurate because they _____ too few people in advance.

5. Last year, the Freedom Party _____ giving medical treatment even to people who could not pay for it.

TOEFL Success   Read the passage to review the vocabulary you have learned. Answer the questions that follow.

In the history of U.S. presidential *elections,* the year 1876 stands out as one of the oddest. That year, *polls* suggested that one person had won the popular vote but another had won more official electoral votes—just as happened in the year 2000. In 1876, however, the election was so *bitterly contested* that a special electoral commission was given the *authority* to determine which *candidate*—Republican Rutherford B. Hayes or Democrat Samuel J. Tilden—had won. This commission represented a *coalition* of interests. The Democrats favored this because otherwise the head of the Senate, Republican Thomas Ferry, would probably have been allowed to declare the winner. In the end, the Democrats were disappointed, as the commission *advocated* the Republican cause. The situation was not settled until March 2 of 1877, only three days before the scheduled *inauguration* of a new president— Hayes, **as it turned out**. Only then did America find out who its new leader would be. Americans seem not to have learned many lessons from 1876, however, because in 2000 there was still no official *policy* on how to settle an election that hung on a few contested votes. The problem was settled (by the Supreme Court) much faster in 2000, but still, no real system had been set up to deal with the situation.

Bonus Structure— **As it turned out** *is an adverbial clause indicating an eventual resolution of a long-standing problem.*

1. In what way was the 1876 election even odder than that in 2000?

   a. It happened much earlier.
   b. It involved only two major candidates.
   c. One person won the popular vote and another won the electoral vote.
   d. The uncertainty over who would win the presidency lasted many months.

2. Who decided the outcome of the 1876 election?

   a. a special electoral commission
   b. Thomas Ferry
   c. the Supreme Court
   d. Rutherford B. Hayes

Lesson 25 Politics

TOEFL Prep I 1. d 2. c 3. b 4. e 5. a
TOEFL Prep II 1. bitterly 2. inaugurated 3. contest 4. polled
   5. advocated
TOEFL Success 1. d 2. a

A Reasonable Doubt

Target Words

1. accuse
2. allegedly
3. civil
4. convict
5. guilty

6. offense
7. peer
8. suspect
9. verdict
10. witness

Definitions and Samples

1. **accuse** *v.*   To say that someone did something wrong (e.g., committed a crime)

    Jordan was **accused** of using a stolen credit card to buy about $300 worth of electronic equipment.

    Usage tips   *Accuse* is often used in the passive voice.

    Parts of speech   accusation *n*, accuser *n*

2. **allegedly** *adv.*   According to what people say

    The chief financial officer of the company **allegedly** took company money for his personal use.

    Parts of speech   allege *v*, allegation *n*

3. **civil** *adj.*   Involving a dispute between two citizens, not a criminal charge

    In a **civil** suit against his neighbor, Barney claimed that the neighbor's dog had bitten him.

Usage tips   In a court context, *civil* almost always appears in one of the following phrases: *civil suit, civil action, civil court, civil proceedings,* and *civil penalties.*

4. **convict** *v.*   To decide that someone is guilty of a crime

Dean was **convicted** of assault after the jury saw a video of him striking another man.

Usage tips   *Convict* is often used in the passive voice.

Parts of speech   convict *n,* conviction *n*

5. **guilty** *adj.*   Responsible for doing something bad

The jury found that the director was **guilty** of embezzlement.

Usage tips   *Guilty* is often followed by an *of* phrase that names a crime or bad deed.

Parts of speech   guilt *n,* guiltily *adv*

6. **offense** *n.*   A specific act that breaks the law

Convicted twice of reckless driving, Victor will lose his license if he commits another serious traffic **offense.**

Parts of speech   offender *n,* offensive *adj*

7. **peer** *n.*   A person who is one's social equal

In requiring judgment by "a jury of one's **peers,**" U.S. law meant to protect lower-class defendants from the possibly biased judgment of upper-class juries.

8. **suspect** *n.*   Someone who, in the opinion of the police, might have committed a certain crime

The police were investigating the activities of five **suspects** in the liquor-store robbery.

Parts of speech   suspect *v,* suspicion *n,* suspicious *adj,* suspiciously *adv*

9. **verdict** *n.*   A judgment in a court case

It took the jury only 30 minutes to reach a **verdict** of "guilty."

Usage tips   *Verdict* is often the object of the verbs *reach* or *arrive at.*

10. **witness** *v.*   To see something, especially a crime, happen

After **witnessing** the car theft, Rodney called the police.

Parts of speech   witness *n*

TOEFL Prep I   Find the word or phrase that is closest in meaning to each word in the left-hand column. Write the letter in the blank.

_____ 1. accuse	(a) to determine that someone is guilty
_____ 2. convict	(b) responsible for a crime
_____ 3. civil	(c) a social equal
_____ 4. guilty	(d) being related to a personal dispute, not a crime
_____ 5. peer	(e) to say someone did a bad thing

TOEFL Prep II   Circle the word that best completes each sentence.

1. The most likely (suspect / witness) in the murder was the victim's brother, but no one actually saw the crime.
2. The new president (allegedly / guiltily) had his main opponents killed, but he denies it.
3. At one time in the United States, possession of marijuana was a minor (verdict / offense).
4. The (witness / peer) made a poor impression on the jury because he couldn't remember many details about the crime scene.
5. Juries are instructed to arrive at a unanimous (verdict / convict), one agreeable to all members of the jury.

TOEFL Success   Read the passage to review the vocabulary you have learned. Answer the questions that follow.

One of the most controversial murder cases of the twentieth century was that involving the death of Marilyn Sheppard in 1954. Her husband, Dr. Sam Sheppard, was *accused* of killing her and then injuring himself. An unlikely *suspect,* Sheppard was highly respected by his *peers* in the medical world. Still, there were odd aspects to the murder that Sheppard could not explain away. Unfortunately for Sheppard, none of his supporters actually *witnessed* the crime, so nobody could back up Sheppard's claim that the real killer was a bushy-haired man whom Sheppard had chased across his lawn and fought with briefly.

Sheppard was eventually *convicted* of the *offense*, **but** many people **doubt**ed the *verdict*. With aggressive help from a lawyer named F. Lee Bailey, Sheppard got a new trial. Bailey suggested many alternatives to Sheppard's guilt, enough that the new jury could not say he was *guilty* beyond a reasonable doubt. Sheppard was released from prison but died soon afterward. His son, Chip, pursued the

> *Bonus Structure—*
> *The clause con-*
> *taining* **but** *and*
> **doubt** *signals*
> *that arguments*
> *against the verdict*
> *will be given.*

case through several *civil* and criminal proceedings in an attempt to find out the truth about his mother's murder. Late in the 1990s, new DNA analysis techniques proved that someone other than Sam Sheppard and his family had been in the house that night. Sheppard's story about the bushy-haired man had probably been accurate all along.

1. Why was the Sheppard case unusual?

    a. A husband was accused of murdering his wife.
    b. The murder occurred in 1954.
    c. Doubt about the guilty verdict led to a second trial.
    d. The accused murderer said he didn't do it.

2. The author of this article implies that Sam Sheppard _____

    a. did not kill his wife
    b. lied about the bushy-haired man
    c. did not love his wife
    d. married again after he got out of prison

Lesson 26　A Reasonable Doubt

TOEFL Prep I　1. e　2. a　3. d　4. b　5. c

TOEFL Prep II　1. suspect　2. allegedly　3. offense　4. witness
5. verdict

TOEFL Success　1. c　2. a

The Police

Target Words

1. apprehend	6. implicate
2. ascertain	7. inquiry
3. bureaucratic	8. intrusively
4. condemn	9. seize
5. evidence	10. surveillance

Definitions and Samples

1. **apprehend** *v.* To capture

    The police **apprehended** the robbery suspect as he tried to get on a bus to Chicago.

    Parts of speech apprehension *n*

2. **ascertain** *v.* To make sure of

    The police failed to **ascertain** that the man they arrested was the Gregory Brown they were really looking for.

    Usage tips *Ascertain* is often followed by a *that* clause. Notice that the root of the word is the adjective *certain,* meaning "sure."

3. **bureaucratic** *adj.* Related to a large organization with a lot of complicated procedures

    Before I could speak with the chief, I had to go through a **bureaucratic** runaround of identity checks and written requests.

Usage tips   *Bureaucratic* implies that something is inefficient and unnecessarily complicated.

Parts of speech   bureaucracy *n*

4. **condemn** *v.*   To speak out against something in very strong terms

Religious radicals **condemned** the government for allowing alcohol to be sold in restaurants.

Parts of speech   condemnation *n*

5. **evidence** *n.*   Something that makes the truth of a statement seem more likely

The most convincing **evidence** that Garner robbed the store was a videotape from surveillance cameras.

Parts of speech   evidence *v*, evident *adj*, evidently *adv*

6. **implicate** *v.*   To suggest that someone was involved in a crime or other wrong behavior

No group claimed responsibility for the bombing, but the type of explosive used **implicates** the Heartland Freedom Militia.

Usage tips   *Implicate* is often followed by *in*.

Parts of speech   implication *n*

7. **inquiry** *n.*   An investigation

The FBI launched an **inquiry** into the relationship between organized crime and the trucking company.

Parts of speech   inquire *v*

8. **intrusively** *adv.*   In a way that brings an unwanted person or thing into someone else's affairs

The new consultant from company headquarters appeared **intrusively** at meetings, staff parties, and other functions where he was not wanted.

Parts of speech   intrude *v*, intrusion *n*, intruder *n*, intrusive *adj*

9. **seize** *v.*   To take something against its owner's will

> Federal agents can **seize** private homes and other property possibly used in the production or sale of illegal drugs.

Parts of speech   seizure *n*

10. **surveillance** *n.*   A process of watching something or someone for a long time, usually because the person is suspected of something

> Police **surveillance** of one suspected car thief resulted in the arrest of a whole gang of carjackers.

Usage tips   *Surveillance* is often followed by an *of* phrase.

TOEFL Prep I   Find the word or phrase that is closest in meaning to the opposite of each word in the left-hand column. Write the letter in the blank.

_____ 1. ascertain	(a) unnoticeably
_____ 2. intrusively	(b) simple and straightforward
_____ 3. seize	(c) give back
_____ 4. condemn	(d) cause doubt about
_____ 5. bureaucratic	(e) praise

TOEFL Prep II   Complete each sentence by filling in the blank with the best word from the list. Change the form of the word if necessary. Use each word only once.

apprehend   evidence   implicate   inquiry   surveillance

1. Officials could not _____ Basil because people in villages and towns throughout the country were willing to hide him.

2. During their _____ of O'Brien's house, detectives audiotaped his phone conversations.

3. Until we finish our _____ into the disappearance of the cash, all employees are suspects.

4. Even if there is _____, such as fingerprints, that might _____ someone in a crime, there might be other indications that the person is innocent.

TOEFL Success   Read the passage to review the vocabulary you have learned. Answer the questions that follow.

The Fourth Amendment to the U.S. Constitution protects citizens from unreasonable search and seizure. Some civil libertarians have *condemned* the federal antidrug *bureaucracy* for threatening this basic right. In a drug case, police need no *evidence* to *intrude* on private property, *apprehend* a suspected dealer, and *seize* all the person's property. Property taken under this law may be sold for a profit later by the law-enforcement officials involved in the raid. The target of a raid might be *implicated* only by an unreliable report from an un-friendly neighbor. The police are not required to *ascertain* whether there's any physical evidence of drug activity at the site. In one case, *surveillance* of a large California property convinced local authorities to seize it—not because they saw drug activity but because the property was worth a lot of money. The property was taken, and its owner was shot trying to defend himself. A later *inquiry* determined that there were no illegal drugs on the property.

Bonus Structure—In one case introduces an example.

1. According to this reading, which of these activities does the author oppose?

   a. marijuana possession
   b. surveillance
   c. property seizures
   d. civil libertarians

2. Why does the author of this reading mention the Fourth Amendment?

   a. because drug-related seizures seem to violate it
   b. because it outlaws the use of certain drugs
   c. because it has finally stopped the antidrug forces from seizing property
   d. because he disagrees that Americans should be protected by it

Lesson 27 The Police

TOEFL Prep I 1. d 2. b 3. e 4. a 5. c
TOEFL Prep II 1. apprehend 2. surveillance 3. inquiry
    4. evidence, implicate
TOEFL Success 1. c 2. a

Investigating Crimes

Target Words

1. analyze
2. assail
3. contrary
4. hypothesize
5. impair

6. inference
7. objectively
8. suspicious
9. tolerate
10. versus

Definitions and Samples

1. **analyze** *v.* To examine something by looking at its parts

   Chemists **analyzed** the white powder and found it to be only a mixture of sugar and salt.

   Parts of speech analysis *n*, analyst *n*

2. **assail** *v.* To attack or criticize forcefully

   With DNA evidence from the crime scene, the defense lawyer **assailed** the police for falsely arresting his client.

   Parts of speech assault *n*, assailant *n*

3. **contrary** *adj.* Opposite

   Contrary to most studies, Dr. Ito's work shows the world's climate is not getting warmer.

   Usage tips Common phrases are *contrary to* and *on the contrary*.

4. **hypothesize** *v.* To make a guess, the correctness of which will eventually be investigated systematically.

Scientists **hypothesize** that planets capable of supporting life exist beyond our solar system, but they have not yet seen any.

Usage tips *Hypothesize* is often followed by a *that* clause.

Parts of speech hypothesis *n*, hypothetical *adj*

5. **impair** *v.* To make something less effective than usual

The snow **impaired** John's ability to hear anyone's footsteps.

Usage tips The object of *impair* is often [*someone's*] *ability to.*

Parts of speech impairment *n*

6. **inference** *n.* A conclusion drawn from evidence

Inspector Dowd's **inference** that Ms. Miller was South African was based on her accent.

Parts of speech infer *v*

7. **objectively** *adv.* Based on unbiased standards, not on personal opinion

I don't like Mr. Rowan, but looking **objectively** at his sales numbers, I saw that he was a very valuable employee.

Parts of speech objective *adj*

8. **suspicious** *adj.* Believing that something is wrong; acting in a way that makes people believe you have done something wrong

The neighbors became **suspicious** of Jim when he bought a big new car and some fancy clothes.

Jim's **suspicious** purchases made his neighbors think he might be getting money illegally.

Parts of speech suspicion *n*, suspiciously *adv*

9. **tolerate** *v.* To avoid getting upset about something

My math teacher **tolerates** a lot of talking in her class, but my history teacher tells us to be quiet.

Parts of speech toleration *n*, tolerance *n*, tolerant *adj*

10. **versus** *prep.*   Against

In the debate, it was pro-war senators **versus** antiwar senators.

Usage tips   *Versus* is often abbreviated as *vs.* in sports contexts, or simply *v.* in legal contexts.

TOEFL Prep I   Find the word or phrase that is closest in meaning to each word in the left-hand column. Write the letter in the blank.

_____ 1. assail	(a) against
_____ 2. contrary	(b) guess
_____ 3. hypothesize	(c) showing differences or opposition
_____ 4. impair	(d) vigorously attack
_____ 5. versus	(e) cause problems for

TOEFL Prep II   Circle the word that best completes each sentence.

1. Most police departments have laboratories, where scientists (assail / analyze) evidence according to scientific procedures.
2. The new police chief would not (tolerate / impair) any joking around in the police station.
3. Everyone assumed Travis was innocent, despite evidence to the (contrary / suspicious).
4. A judge who feels unable to think (versus / objectively) about a case should withdraw from it.
5. The bomb squad was called after a (suspicious / contrary) package was delivered to the governor's office.

TOEFL Success   Read the passage to review the vocabulary you have learned. Answer the questions that follow.

Bonus Structure— **This** *refers to the whole situation described in the previous sentence, not to any one noun phrase.*

In 1979, two British farmers reported that, while sitting on a hill, they suddenly saw the crops below flattened in a perfect circle. They *inferred* that some great force must have come down directly from above to squash the corn and barley. **This** started a public hysteria about so-called crop circles. The patterns pressed into the crops (not all of them were circles) seemed to have no entry or exit points. Many people *hypothesized* that only alien spaceships could make such bizarre imprints. Others, including Britain's police, *assailed* such wild conclusions. They had a *contrary* theory: Someone was playing a big hoax. Teams of investigators took samples of the plants and the soil, trying to *objectively analyze* the crop circles as if they were a crime scene. Public curiosity often *impaired* the investigators, who had to *tolerate* busloads of tourists flocking to the circles. The farmers in the area, long *suspicious* of the police, approached the case as an instance of police *versus* the people. If the local farmers knew the circles were a hoax, they wouldn't say so.

1. According to the article, why did many people think that crop circles were created by alien spaceships?

   a. The circles looked like they had been made from above and had no way in or out.
   b. The observers in 1979 reported seeing a UFO land and make a crop circle.
   c. The plants and soil inside a crop circle contained chemicals not found on Earth.
   d. They were in unusual shapes and contained alien symbols.

2. Why does the author mention "a hoax"?

   a. because one of the locals admitted playing a trick on his neighbors
   b. because most people think that crop circles are evil
   c. because police investigators thought crop circles were made by humans as a joke
   d. because crop circles are probably made by secret government aircraft

Lesson 28   Investigating Crimes

TOEFL Prep I   1. d   2. c   3. b   4. e   5. a
TOEFL Prep II   1. analyze   2. tolerate   3. contrary
   4. objectively   5. suspicious
TOEFL Success   1. a   2. c

Government Corruption

Target Words

1. bribery
2. cynically
3. erode
4. evade
5. grotesque

6. integrity
7. prevalent
8. reform
9. scandal
10. unmask

Definitions and Samples

1. **bribery** *n.* Giving money or other gifts to a government official or other person in authority in order to get special privileges

   Bribery of police officers is common in countries where police salaries are very low.

   Parts of speech bribe *v*, bribe *n*

2. **cynically** *adv.* Disrespectfully; emphasizing the weaknesses of otherwise respected things

   Employees of the Roadways Department **cynically** referred to their boss as "the banker" because he took so many bribes.

   Parts of speech cynic *n*, cynicism *n*, cynical *adj*

3. **erode** *v.* To wear away and become smaller

   People's respect for the government **eroded** as more officials were arrested for corruption.

Usage tips   *Erode* can be intransitive (*the beach eroded*) or transitive (*the waves eroded the beach*).

Parts of speech   erosion *n,* erosive *adj*

4. **evade** *v.*   To get away from something that tries to catch you

The robbery suspects tried to **evade** the police by fleeing to Canada.

Parts of speech   evasion *n,* evasive *adj*

5. **grotesque** *adj.*   Extremely unattractive, in a way that catches a lot of attention.

Spending $3.5 million to redecorate the governor's house is a **grotesque** misuse of public money.

6. **integrity** *n.*   Personal honesty and good character

We don't have a problem with our employees stealing from the store because we hire only people with a lot of **integrity.**

7. **prevalent** *adj.*   Common; easy to find because it exists in great amounts

Distrust of elected officials was **prevalent** in our county because many of them were friends with certain candidates.

Parts of speech   prevail *v,* prevalence *n*

8. **reform** *v.*   To make big improvements

The new law was an attempt to **reform** the system of giving money to political candidates.

Parts of speech   reform *n,* reformer *n*

9. **scandal** *n.*   A case of wrongdoing that hurts someone's reputation

In the Watergate **scandal,** some of the president's top advisors were revealed to be criminals.

Parts of speech   scandalize *v,* scandalous *adj*

10. **unmask** *v.*   Reveal; expose something that is hidden

The Forge Trucking Company was eventually **unmasked** as a front for organized crime.

TOEFL Prep I Find the word or phrase that is closest in meaning to the opposite of each word in the left-hand column. Write the letter in the blank.

_____ 1. cynically   (a) respectfully
_____ 2. evade   (b) corruption
_____ 3. integrity   (c) cover up
_____ 4. prevalent   (d) uncommon
_____ 5. unmask   (e) get caught

TOEFL Prep II Circle the word that best completes each sentence.

1. The president resigned because a (scandal / bribery) made it impossible for him to lead.
2. Laws that let the police monitor criminals can (erode / evade) the privacy of innocent citizens too.
3. After Downforth Castle was bought by apartment developers, it became a (prevalent / grotesque) jumble of poorly built additions.
4. In some places, people who are pulled over for traffic offenses use (scandal / bribery) to avoid getting a ticket.
5. President Carazza came to office promising (reform / integrity) of the prison system.

TOEFL Success Read the passage to review the vocabulary you have learned. Answer the questions that follow.

In many countries, few politicians have enough *integrity* to resist corruption and *bribery*. Because such practices are so *prevalent,* officials often *evade* any personal sense of guilt by pretending that everyone is just as corrupt as they are. Even in cases of really *grotesque* corruption, the kind that might cause a *scandal* in a less-corrupt government, the general population may not be shocked. Instead, they may *cynically* conclude that government corruption is natural and unavoidable. **In this environment,** the efforts of an honest politician to *unmask* corruption may be *eroded* by the public's lack of interest, causing any efforts at *reform* to fail.

Bonus Structure— **In this environment** *means "under these conditions."*

1. Why do people in some countries not react negatively to corruption?

    a. because they feel it cannot be avoided
    b. because they want reform
    c. because almost everyone in the government is corrupt
    d. because they have paid money to gain influence

2. What effect might a small scandal have in a country where government corruption is not typical?

    a. It could make someone very popular.
    b. It could cause a politician to become cynical.
    c. It could cost a lot of money.
    d. It could cause a government official to lose his or her position.

Lesson 29   Government Corruption

TOEFL Prep I   1. a   2. e   3. b   4. d   5. c
TOEFL Prep II   1. scandal   2. erode   3. grotesque   4. bribery
    5. reform
TOEFL Success   1. c   2. d

Crimes at Sea

Target Words

1. abduction
2. coerce
3. detain
4. deviant
5. distort
6. intentionally
7. piracy
8. predicament
9. smuggle
10. villainy

Definitions and Samples

1. **abduction** *n.* Kidnapping

   Pirates got many crew members by **abduction,** snatching unlucky citizens from seaport towns.

   Parts of speech abduct *v*

2. **coerce** *v.* To force; to put pressure on someone to do something

   A criminal's confession is not usable in court if the police **coerce** him or her into giving it.

   Parts of speech coercion *n*, coercive *adj*

3. **detain** *v.* To prevent someone, for a relatively short time, from going on their way

   The police **detained** at least 20 men for questioning, but charged none of them with a crime.

   Parts of speech detention *n*, detainee *n*

4. **deviant** *adj.*   In a style that is not normal and is offensive to many

The artist based his reputation on creating **deviant** works of art that disgusted most of the public.

Usage tips   *Deviant* always implies a bad opinion of someone or something.

Parts of speech   deviant *n*, deviation *n*, deviate *v*

5. **distort** *v.*   To twist or misrepresent; to make something seem different from what it really is

If you hold a pencil in a glass of water, the water **distorts** the appearance of the pencil.

Parts of speech   distortion *n*

6. **intentionally** *adv.*   On purpose, not by accident

Danny **intentionally** lost his last golf ball because he was tired of playing.

Parts of speech   intent *n*, intention *n*. intend *v*, intentional *adj*

7. **piracy** *n.*   Stealing a ship or taking the ship's cargo; the unlawful copying of books, CDs, etc.

Modern-day **piracy** occurs mostly near groups of small, uninhabited islands where pirates can hide.

The software company constantly battled **piracy.**

Parts of speech   pirate *n*, pirate *v*

8. **predicament** *n.*   A difficult situation, one that is hard to get out of

College basketball stars face the **predicament** of wanting to graduate but being tempted by high professional salaries.

9. **smuggle** *v.*   To illegally bring things into a country

The pirate Ben Dewar **smuggled** guns to British and Indian fighters in North America.

Parts of speech   smuggler *n*, smuggling *n*

10. **villainy** *n.*   Exceptional badness, as demonstrated by many serious evil
    deeds

    Fred was not a natural criminal, but he learned all kinds of **villainy**
    while being jailed for a minor crime.

    Parts of speech   villain *n*, villainous *adj*

TOEFL Prep I   Find the word or phrase that is closest in meaning
to the opposite of each word in the left-hand column. Write the letter in the blank.

_____ 1. detain	(a)	clarify
_____ 2. distort	(b)	by accident
_____ 3. villainy	(c)	let go
_____ 4. intentionally	(d)	normal
_____ 5. deviant	(e)	good deeds

TOEFL Prep II   Choose the word from the list that is closest in
meaning to the underlined part of each sentence. Write it in the
blank.

abducted   coerced   piracy   predicament   smuggled

_____ 1. The police force's <u>difficult situation</u> involved a bank rob-
ber who threatened to shoot a bank employee if any po-
lice approached.

_____ 2. Despite laws restricting animal imports, thousands of
monkeys and lemurs and other wild animals are
<u>brought illegally</u> into the United States.

_____ 3. The enemy <u>captured and took away</u> the general's son.

_____ 4. Two men were convicted of <u>stealing a boat</u> near the Riau
Islands.

_____ 5. By threatening to set fire to their ship, the governor of
Bermuda <u>pressured</u> the pirate crew to give themselves up.

TOEFL Success Read the passage to review the vocabulary you have learned. Answer the question that follows.

The Spanish explorer Pizarro's *abduction* of the Inca King Atahualpa came in 1529. His men *detained* the king, *coerced* the Incas into paying a large ransom in gold and silver, and then *intentionally* killed the king anyway. Their conquest of Peru established the legendary Spanish Main — Spanish holdings on the mainland of Central and South America. The *predicament* for Spain's kings was how to get the riches of the New World to Spain. Pirates and privateers ruled the waves. To *distort* what was actually just robbery, the king of England issued "letters of marque," licenses that turned certain pirates into agents of the British government. Their *piracy* against Spanish ships and Spanish gold was considered service to the king or queen of England.

Most pirates with such letters were social *deviants* anyway, and **predictably,** they became embarrassments to the British crown. In 1603, Britain's King James I canceled all his government's letters of marque. The many dangerous, unemployed pirates became buccaneers, a terrifying mix of tough characters that operated from the island of Hispaniola. They conducted merciless raids on Spanish settlements and formed a brotherhood known for theft, torture, *smuggling,* and *villainy* of all sorts.

> **Bonus Structure—Predictably** *means that the information that follows is no surprise.*

An introductory sentence for a brief summary of the passage is provided below. Complete the summary by selecting three answer choices that express the most important ideas in the passage. In each blank, write the letter of one of your choices.

> The establishment of the Spanish Main provided rich targets for pirates and privateers, often with government encouragement.
>
> •
> •
> •

a. Pizarro's men abducted King Atahualpa in 1529.
b. By issuing letters of marque, the kings of England gave their approval of raids on Spanish ships.
c. Piracy in the South China Sea was also a problem at this time.
d. Pirates who worked for the English crown were known as buccaneers.
e. Sailing under a letter of marque, a privateer could steal property in the king's name.
f. Eventually, the English crown was embarrassed by the behavior of its privateers and canceled the letters of marque.

Lesson 30   Crimes at Sea

TOEFL Prep I   1. c   2. a   3. e   4. b   5. d
TOEFL Prep II   1. predicament   2. smuggled   3. abducted
    4. piracy   5. coerced
TOEFL Success   b, e, f

The War on Drugs

Target Words

1. addictive	6. misconception
2. cartel	7. modify
3. concentrated	8. potent
4. interdict	9. residual
5. juxtapose	10. subtly

Definitions and Samples

1. **addictive** *adj.*   Making someone want it so much that the person feels ill without it

   Some drugs, like heroin or methamphetamines, are **addictive** to almost everyone who tries them.

   Parts of speech   addict *v*, addict *n*, addiction *n*

2. **cartel** *n.*   A small group controlling a certain area of business

   The world's major oil producers formed a **cartel** to control the price and supply of petroleum.

3. **concentrated** *adj.*   Strong because large amounts are in a certain space

   Concentrated lemon juice is very sour, so I mix it with water when I make lemonade.

   Parts of speech   concentrate *v*, concentration *n*, concentrate *n*

4. **interdict** *v.* To keep something from reaching a certain place

With faster patrol boats, the Coast Guard can more easily **interdict** drugs being smuggled by sea.

Parts of speech interdiction *n*

5. **juxtapose** *v.* Place next to one another

If you **juxtapose** these two similar flowers, you can see clear differences between them.

Parts of speech juxtaposition *n*

6. **misconception** *n.* A mistaken belief

A common **misconception** about rabbits is that they are a kind of rodent.

7. **modify** *v.* Make small changes in order to get a certain result

People who live in high mountains often **modify** their car engines to run well in the thinner air.

Parts of speech modification *n,* modifier *n*

8. **potent** *adj.* Powerful

A very **potent** type of marijuana with surprisingly strong effects became available in Burrytown.

Parts of speech potency *n*

9. **residual** *adj.* Left behind after most of a thing has gone

In the airplane, agents found **residual** traces of heroin.

Usage tips *Residual* is often followed by *trace, amount,* or some other word referring to "quantity."

Parts of speech residue *n*

10. **subtly** *adv.* In a quiet, hard-to-notice way

By **subtly** changing the soft drink's formula, we improved its taste and made production cheaper.

Parts of speech subtlety *n,* subtle *adj*

TOEFL Prep I Find the word or phrase that is closest in meaning to each word in the left-hand column. Write the letter in the blank.

_____ 1. cartel   (a) stop
_____ 2. interdict   (b) remaining
_____ 3. juxtaposed   (c) next to
_____ 4. residual   (d) without drawing attention
_____ 5. subtle   (e) a kind of group

TOEFL Prep II Circle the word that best completes each sentence.

1. With a (subtle / residual) nod of his head, the inspector signaled his agents.
2. Sunlight is a (concentrated / potent) source of energy for electricity generation, but it can be expensive to collect and store.
3. Things other than drugs can be (addictive / subtle), such as gambling or even television.
4. A security official tries to (modify / interdict) foreign terrorists before they can enter the country.
5. Your advertisement created the (misconception / cartel) that everything was on sale for 50 percent off.

TOEFL Success Read the passage to review the vocabulary you have learned. Answer the questions that follow.

Illegal *addictive* drugs, like heroin or cocaine, come from plants grown and harvested mostly by poor farmers. Their small farmhouses *juxtaposed* with the mansions of billionaire drug lords illustrate the unequal payouts to various players in the drug trade. The farmers sell their product cheaply to a drug-distribution *cartel* that is owned by the drug lords. People working for the cartel **then** refine the drugs into a *concentrated* form, or even *modify* them chemically to make them more *potent* and therefore more valuable. Other cartel members **then** transport the drugs to distributors for sale, smuggling them over huge distances, including international borders. Governments try to *interdict* smugglers, using both

> *Bonus Structure—*
> *Because this reading describes a system of operations, the word* then *appears very often.*

new technology and old (like sniffer dogs) to find *residual* traces of drugs. Their occasional successes have led to a popular *misconception* that antidrug campaigns are close to stopping the flow of illegal drugs. On the contrary, as long as drug lords can make vast fortunes in their illegal trade, smugglers will come up with ever-more-*subtle* ways of concealing their goods, and the War on Drugs goes on.

1. Who makes the most money from the drug trade?

     a. rural farmers

     b. people who refine drugs

     c. drug lords

     d. antidrug officers

2. Schematic table: Write the letter of each phrase in either column A or column B, based on which one it relates to according to the reading.

A. Drug producers and dealers	B. Antidrug forces

     a. subtle ways of hiding drugs

     b. sniffer dogs

     c. high-tech detection

     d. concentrate drugs to make them potent

     e. pay farmers to grow plants that yield drugs

Lesson 31   The War on Drugs

TOEFL Prep I   1. e   2. a   3. c   4. b   5. d

TOEFL Prep II   1. subtle   2. potent   3. addictive   4. interdict
     5. misconception

TOEFL Success   1. c   2. Column A: a, d, e   Column B: b, c

Relationships

Family Relationships

Target Words

1. ancestral	6. legitimate
2. cohesion	7. paternal
3. descendant	8. proximity
4. inheritance	9. sentiment
5. kin	10. sibling

Definitions and Samples

1. **ancestral** *adj.* Relating to family members from earlier generations

   Sweden is my **ancestral** homeland, from which my great-grandfather emigrated in 1922.

   Parts of speech ancestor *n*, ancestry *n*

2. **cohesion** *n.* Ability to stay together as a unit

   Family **cohesion** is difficult if young people have to go far away to find work.

   Usage tips *Cohesion* can also be used to describe forces that keep materials or structures together.

   Parts of speech cohere *v*, cohesiveness *n*

3. **descendant** *n.* A direct relative in a later generation (such as one's son, daughter, or grandchild)

Billy Sobieski claimed to be a **descendant** of Jan Sobieski, a former king of Poland.

Usage tips   *Descendant* is often followed by an *of* phrase.

Parts of speech   descend *v*, descent *n*

4. **inheritance** *n.*   Things passed down to you from your ancestors

My **inheritance** from my grandmother included her favorite necklace.

Parts of speech   inherit *v*, inheritor *n*

5. **kin** *n.*   Relatives

Even though my uncle didn't really like me, he was kind to me because we were **kin.**

Usage tips   A common phrase is *next of kin,* meaning "closest relative."

Parts of speech   kinship *n*

6. **legitimate** *adj.*   True and respectable; in the context of family, born of a mother and father who were married to each other

You can skip the meeting if you have a **legitimate** reason.

Harcourt had two legitimate children with his wife Hannah and one **illegitimate** son with a woman whom he met while traveling.

Usage tips   The opposite of *legitimate* is *illegitimate.*

Parts of speech   legitimize *v*, legitimacy *n*

7. **paternal** *adj.*   Relating to a father

My mother's parents have both died, but my **paternal** grandparents are still alive.

Usage tips   *Paternal* may appear with *maternal,* meaning "relating to a mother."

8. **proximity** *n.*   Nearness

The house was comfortable, except for its **proximity** to a busy road.

Usage tips *Proximity* can be followed by an *of* phrase or a *to* phrase.

Parts of speech proximate *adj*

9. **sentiment** *n.* Feelings; opinion based on feelings

   I share your **sentiments** about air travel, but I disagree that cars are safer.

   Usage tips *Sentiments* (the plural) is more common than *sentiment.*

   Parts of speech sentimentality *n,* sentimental *adj*

10. **sibling** *n.* Brother or sister

    My **siblings** and I got together to buy our parents a gift for their anniversary.

    Usage tips *Sibling* is often preceded by a possessive noun or pronoun.

TOEFL Prep I Find the word or phrase that is closest in meaning to each word in the left-hand column. Write the letter in the blank.

_____ 1. ancestral	(a) fatherly
_____ 2. descendants	(b) children, grandchildren, etc.
_____ 3. legitimate	(c) what one thinks or feels
_____ 4. paternal	(d) acceptable and right
_____ 5. sentiments	(e) related to earlier generations

TOEFL Prep II Complete each sentence by filling in the blank with the best word from the list. Change the form of the word if necessary. Use each word only once.

cohesion   inheritance   kin   proximity   siblings

1. You can't expect to have family _____ if the members don't respect each other.

2. In our family, the _____ who are closest in age get along the best.

3. If someone dies without a will, the possessions usually go to the next of _____.

4. Medical bills in his last year greatly reduced the _____ going to Tom's wife.

5. Legally, parents have the same _____ of relationship to an adopted child as to their biological children.

TOEFL Success   Read the passage to review the vocabulary you have learned. Answer the questions that follow.

The nature of the family varies widely from culture to culture. In some societies, family members tend to stay in close *proximity* to their *kin*, never moving more than a few miles away from the *ancestral* home. In other places, while the members of one generation may all live near one another, their *descendants* in the next generation scatter widely. In such a case, it's difficult to maintain the same family *cohesion* enjoyed by those who live close together. Sometimes marriage can govern family structure; for example, there may be strict traditions requiring a new bride to leave her *paternal* home and *siblings* to move in with her new husband's family. Such traditions are followed, even by young couples who don't like them, because going against them is likely to result in the loss of *inheritance*. Whatever one's own *sentiments* about family structure, it is important to recognize that one culture's family system is as *legitimate* as another's.

1. Which of the following best states the main idea of this passage?

   a. Different family systems can be found worldwide, but each one deserves respect.
   b. Societies in which children move far away from their parents are not very cohesive.
   c. Although some societies still require a wife to move in with her husband's family, this tradition is dying out.
   d. The most important factor in family happiness is close proximity to your relatives.

2. According to this reading, which family system is most common?

   a. Members of a family living in the same community.
   b. Family members spreading out and living in various cities.
   c. Young couples living with the man's parents.
   d. It is impossible to tell from this reading.

Lesson 32 Family Relationships

TOEFL Prep I 1. e 2. b 3. d 4. a 5. c

TOEFL Prep II 1. cohesion 2. siblings 3. kin 4. inheritance
5. proximity

TOEFL Success 1. a 2. d

Friendship

Target Words

1. affection	6. exclusive
2. associate	7. fluctuate
3. bond	8. in common
4. clique	9. solidarity
5. confide	10. willing

Definitions and Samples

1. **affection** *n.* An emotional closeness or warmth

   I show **affection** for my girlfriend by spending time with her, not by spending money on her.

   Usage tips *Affection* is often followed by a *for* phrase.

   Parts of speech affectionate *adj*

2. **associate** *v.* To regularly spend time together

   Carol doesn't **associate** with people who smoke.

   Usage tips *Associate* is often followed by a *with* phrase.

   Parts of speech association *n*, associate *n*

3. **bond** *n.* A close connection

   Some researchers say that there is an especially strong emotional **bond** between twins.

Usage tips   A *between* phrase—indicating the things that are connected—often follows *bond*.

Parts of speech   bond *v*

4. **clique** *n.*   A small group of friends who are unfriendly to people outside the group

High-schoolers form **cliques** to gain security and acceptance.

Usage tips   *Clique* indicates a negative feeling toward a group.

Parts of speech   cliquish *adj*

5. **confide** *v.*   To tell very personal things

Teenagers are more willing to **confide** in a friend than in a parent.

Usage tips   *Confide* is almost always followed by an *in* phrase.

Parts of speech   confidence *n,* confidant *n,* confidential *adj*

6. **exclusive** *adj.*   Keeping out all but a few people

The most **exclusive** universities accept only a small percentage of people who want to attend.

Usage tips   *Exclusive* can indicate a positive opinion, but in the context of friendship, it can mean "attached only to one person."

Parts of speech   exclude *v,* exclusion *n,* exclusively *adv*

7. **fluctuate** *v.*   To change often, from one condition to another

Earth's climate **fluctuates** between warm periods and cold periods.

Usage tips   *Fluctuate* is usually followed by a *between* phrase (or by a *from . . . to* structure).

Parts of speech   fluctuation *n*

8. **in common** *adv.*   As a shared characteristic

Billy and Heather have a lot **in common**—basketball, a love of pizza, and an interest in snakes.

Usage tips   *In common* very often appears with the verb *to have.*

9. **solidarity** *n.*   Standing together despite pressure to move apart

Many student groups declared **solidarity** with the Latino Student Association in their effort to get a Spanish-speaking principal.

Usage tips   *Solidarity* is usually used in political contexts.

10. **willing** *adj.*   Agreeable and ready to do something

Because of their long friendship, Professor Gardner was **willing** to say a few words at Jones's birthday celebration.

Usage tips   *Willing* is almost always followed by a *to* + verb structure.

Parts of speech   will *v*, will *n*, willingness *n*

TOEFL Prep I   Find the word or phrase that is closest in meaning to each word in the left-hand column. Write the letter in the blank.

_____ 1. affection
_____ 2. bond
_____ 3. clique
_____ 4. fluctuate
_____ 5. solidarity

(a) liking someone or something
(b) to move back and forth
(c) standing together in a political cause
(d) a connection
(e) an exclusive group

TOEFL Prep II   Circle the word or phrase that best completes each sentence.

1. Charles is (exclusive / willing) to be friends with Dory, but he is already dating another girl.
2. If I (associate / confide) in you, do you promise to keep what I say a secret?
3. When it comes to weather, Minnesota and North Dakota have a lot (in common / in a bond).
4. One of the main reasons to go to an exclusive college is that you get to (associate / fluctuate) with some of the country's future leaders.
5. The court said that the club's membership rules were unjustly (willing / exclusive) because they kept out people of certain ethnic groups.

TOEFL Success   Read the passage to review the vocabulary you have learned. Answer the questions that follow.

You can walk into any high school and spot the *cliques:* the jocks hang out here, the geeks there, the Goths and preppies in their areas. Teenagers feel a strong need to belong to a group, to *associate* with people with whom they share common interests or goals. Since adolescence is often a time when teens feel turmoil in their home lives, they seek *affection* and friendship outside the home. They look for other young people to *bond* with when their parents don't seem to "understand." Teens going through the various crises of adolescence can more easily *confide* in others their own age, with whom they have more *in common.* Teen cliques are by no means *exclusive*; membership can *fluctuate* on an almost daily basis, but the important thing is that group members feel a sense of *solidarity* and are *willing* to stick together.

1. According to the reading, why do adolescents search for friendship outside the home?

   a. They want to be accepted by the jocks and Goths.
   b. They think their parents don't understand the problems they face.
   c. They want to be in a different clique every day.
   d. They want to talk about their parents with other teenagers.

2. According to the reading, do teens stay in the same groups all the time?

   a. Yes, because their parents want them to.
   b. Yes, because they share common interests.
   c. No, they may move from group to group quite frequently.
   d. No, most groups don't accept new members.

Lesson 33   Friendship

TOEFL Prep I   1. a   2. d   3. e   4. b   5. c
TOEFL Prep II   1. willing   2. confide   3. in common
      4. associate   5. exclusive
TOEFL Success   1. b   2. c

Passion

Target Words

1. complex
2. despondent
3. devotion
4. dilemma
5. engender

6. loyal
7. passion
8. proliferation
9. reciprocity
10. vanish

Definitions and Samples

1. **complex** *adj.*   Not simple; involving many parts that work together

   A modern car engine is too **complex** for most car owners to repair by themselves.

   Parts of speech   complexity *n*

2. **despondent** *adj.*   Extremely sad and without hope for the future

   After his girlfriend left him, Johnson was **despondent** and wouldn't talk to anyone.

3. **devotion** *n.*   A willingness to keep supporting someone you admire

   Grant showed great **devotion** to his wife, supporting her during her long illness.

   Usage tips   *Devotion* is often followed by a *to* phrase.

   Parts of speech   devote *v*, devotee *n*

4. **dilemma** *n.* A difficult choice between two things

I was caught in a **dilemma** between traveling by airplane and taking a train, which is slower but more comfortable.

5. **engender** *v.* To bring into being; to cause to exist

The government's warnings about terrorism **engendered** fear throughout the nation.

Usage tips *Engender* is often followed by a noun for an emotion.

6. **loyal** *adj.* Faithful

Carter was **loyal** to his girlfriend and would not date anyone else.

Usage tips *Loyal* is often followed by a *to* phrase.

Parts of speech loyalty *n*, loyally *adv*

7. **passion** *n.* An extremely strong emotion, like love or anger

Debbie complained that there was no **passion** in her marriage.

Parts of speech passionate *adj*, passionately *adv*

8. **proliferation** *n.* An increase in the number of something and in the number of places it can be found

The **proliferation** of fast-food restaurants has made it harder for Americans to eat healthy lunches.

Usage tips *Proliferation* is very often followed by an *of* phrase.

Parts of speech proliferate *v*

9. **reciprocity** *n.* Doing as much for another as he or she has done for you

Dan was giving a lot of attention to Kelly, but he felt no **reciprocity** in their relationship.

Parts of speech reciprocate *v*, reciprocal *adj*

10. **vanish** *v.* To disappear suddenly

When the sun came out, last night's light snowfall **vanished.**

TOEFL Prep I   Find the word or phrase that is closest in meaning to the opposite of each word in the left-hand column. Write the letter in the blank.

_____ 1. complex	(a) an easy choice
_____ 2. dilemma	(b) simple
_____ 3. loyal	(c) a decrease
_____ 4. proliferation	(d) appear
_____ 5. vanish	(e) unfaithful

TOEFL Prep II   Choose the word from the list that is closest in meaning to the underlined part of each sentence. Write it in the blank.

despondent   devotion to   engender   passion   reciprocity

_____ 1. In a good relationship, there is a lot of <u>give and take</u>.

_____ 2. Mr. Foster's <u>strong love</u> for teaching makes him successful.

_____ 3. Rhonda was <u>extremely sad</u> after the death of her cat.

_____ 4. Sometimes, a small characteristic, like a nice smile, can <u>cause</u> love.

_____ 5. My <u>continuing support for</u> the candidate is based on my admiration for her.

TOEFL Success   Read the passage to review the new vocabulary you have learned. Answer the questions that follow.

Perhaps no emotion is more complex than *passion*. Passion can show itself in a negative way as a burst of anger, or in a more pleasant way, as love. Passion can *engender* blind *devotion* for a lover or plunge a person into *despondent* misery if he or she feels a lack of *reciprocity* in the relationship. Passion and love cause innumerable *dilemmas*, and people constantly seek out ways to understand these emotions, as evidenced by the *proliferation* of articles, books, talk shows, and Web pages devoted to relationships. Many of these forums have *loyal* followings and have become cultural fixtures. The endless flow of information and opinions about the *complex* situations aroused by passion will probably not *vanish* anytime soon.

1. According to this article, which statement about passion is true?
    a. It can have good or bad effects.
    b. It can be easily explained.
    c. It helps people decide what to do.
    d. It is irrational.

2. According to the reading, why are there so many books and other works about passion?
    a. because people want a lot of advice about love
    b. because many people want to write about their own passion
    c. because reading about passion is relaxing
    d. because passion can also show itself as a burst of anger

Lesson 34   Passion

TOEFL Prep I   1. b   2. a   3. e   4. c   5. d
TOEFL Prep II   1. reciprocity   2. passion   3. despondent
    4. engender   5. devotion to
TOEFL Success   1. a   2. a

Negative Emotions

Target Words

1. antipathy
2. arrogantly
3. berate
4. contemptuous
5. despise

6. humiliation
7. obnoxious
8. shame
9. stigmatize
10. vitriolic

Definitions and Samples

1. **antipathy** *n.*   A strong, long-lasting negative feeling

    My **antipathy** toward telemarketers is so strong that I am often rude to them.

    Usage tips   *Antipathy* is often followed by a *toward* phrase.

2. **arrogantly** *adv.*   In a way that shows a high opinion of oneself and a low opinion of others

    Jenny told us about her party only one day in advance, **arrogantly** thinking we had nothing else to do.

    Parts of speech   arrogance *n*, arrogant *adj*

3. **berate** *v.*   To say insulting and disrespectful things

    The teacher lost his job because he cruelly **berated** students who made mistakes.

Usage tips You can only berate someone directly—only when he or she can hear you.

4. **contemptuous** *n.* Having no respect

Most scientists are **contemptuous** of reports that aliens from outer space have landed on the Earth.

Usage tips A very common structure is *be contemptuous of.*

Parts of speech contempt *n,* contemptible *adj,* contemptuously *adv*

5. **despise** *v.* Hate very much

Tom grew to **despise** his greedy and unfriendly boss.

6. **humiliation** *n.* An event that causes someone to feel that she or he has lost the respect of others

Losing the chess tournament was a great **humiliation** for Marie, and she never played chess again.

Parts of speech humiliate *v*

7. **obnoxious** *adj.* Bothersome; doing small things that others don't like

My **obnoxious** neighbor keeps talking to me while I'm trying to read in my backyard.

Parts of speech obnoxiously *adv*

8. **shame** *n.* Dishonor because one has done something wrong

Feeling deep **shame** because of their son's crimes, the Ford family moved to a different town.

Usage tips *Shame* is often followed by an *of* or *about* phrase.

Parts of speech shame *v,* shameful *adj,* ashamed *adj,* shamefully *adv*

9. **stigmatize** *v.* To mark with a visible feature that makes other people think, perhaps incorrectly, that someone or something is wrong

Cadbury's beard and tattoos **stigmatized** him as a bad match for Wall Street, so he couldn't find work as a financial analyst.

Parts of speech stigma *n*

10. **vitriolic** *adj.*   Showing an extreme, hateful anger

   The mayor's **vitriolic** attacks against the city council only made him sound unreasonable.

   Usage tips   The origin of *vitriolic* is "vitriol," a strong chemical that could cause painful burns.

TOEFL Prep I   Find the word or phrase that is closest in meaning to each word in the left-hand column. Write the letter in the blank.

_____ 1. arrogantly	(a) very bitter and hurtful
_____ 2. berate	(b) to criticize and insult
_____ 3. humiliation	(c) annoying
_____ 4. obnoxious	(d) too proudly
_____ 5. vitriolic	(e) embarrassment

TOEFL Prep II   Circle the word that best completes each sentence. Be careful: Many words in this chapter are very close in meaning to each other. Pay attention to small details in order to choose the best.

1. As a teenager, Dean did a lot of stupid things that he now feels (humiliation / shame) about.
2. Many foreigners feel that their appearance (stigmatizes / despises) them in this country.
3. Because the president was (obnoxious / contemptuous) of France's opinion long ago, the French are not eager to help him now.
4. Mark (despises / berates) Henry and refuses to see him at all.
5. Turkey's historic (antipathy / shame) toward Greece may be softening with the new generation.

TOEFL Success   Read the passage to review the vocabulary you have learned. Answer the questions that follow.

Some radio talk show hosts are masters of *obnoxious* insults. Callers to such shows should be prepared for *humiliation* if they dare to disagree with the host's views. The host controls whether the caller can speak, so he can *arrogantly berate* the caller without allowing the caller to respond. Some shows, especially on AM radio, have hosts who are *contemptuous* of nearly everyone. They regularly use *vitriolic* language to *stigmatize* whole groups of people, such as foreigners, liberals, gays, or women. Some hosts don't actually *despise* the groups they insult. They simply use *antipathy* as a form of entertainment, and they seem to feel no *shame* about the damage they do.

1. Which phrase best describes the author's point of view?

   a. The author enjoys listening to radio talk shows.
   b. The author believes talk shows can cause damage.
   c. The author thinks talk show hosts are disturbing but honest.
   d. The author argues that hosts are ordinary people just doing their jobs.

2. Which people are often berated on radio talk shows, according to the author?

   a. hosts
   b. callers
   c. listeners
   d. advertisers

Lesson 35 Negative Emotions

TOEFL Prep I   1. d   2. b   3. e   4. c   5. a
TOEFL Prep II   1. shame   2. stigmatizes   3. contemptuous
   4. despises   5. antipathy
TOEFL Success   1. b   2. b

Culture

Social Rebels

Target Words

1. adolescent
2. cause
3. conflict
4. delinquency
5. fringe

6. hedonistic
7. hypocritically
8. manipulation
9. rebel
10. status quo

Definitions and Samples

1. **adolescent** *adj.* Characteristic of a teenager; not fully grown up

   In policy meetings, George refuses to reason with anyone and just scowls in an **adolescent** way.

   Parts of speech adolescent *n,* adolescence *n*

2. **cause** *n.* A political or social goal that one believes is right and works to achieve

   Our river cleanup effort would be more effective if someone famous spoke out for the **cause.**

3. **conflict** *v.* To fit so poorly together that the differences cause a problem

   A teenager's need for security can **conflict** with his desire for independence from his family.

   Parts of speech conflict *n*

4. **delinquency** *n.*   Serious misbehavior; not doing what one should do

   Because of his laziness and **delinquency,** Lefty was an unreliable friend.

   Usage tips   A common combination is *juvenile delinquency,* meaning "criminal behavior by a teenager."

   Parts of speech   delinquent *n,* delinquent *adj*

5. **fringe** *n.*   Edge; in social contexts, parts of society that look or act very different from most people

   Punk music got its start at the **fringe** of London's rock music culture.

   Usage tips   *Fringe* implies an edge that is uneven and not very solid.

   Parts of speech   fringy *adj*

6. **hedonistic** *adj.*   Excessively interested in seeking pleasure

   Suddenly wealthy, Allen fell into a **hedonistic** life of parties, expensive dinners, and heavy drinking.

   Usage tips   *Hedonistic* usually implies that the pleasures are wrong.

   Parts of speech   hedonist *n,* hedonism *n,* hedonistically *adv*

7. **hypocritically** *adv.*   In a way that accuses other people of weaknesses that the speaker also possesses

   Henry spent $2,500 on a new suit and then **hypocritically** accused me of spending too much on clothes.

   Parts of speech   hypocrite *n,* hypocrisy *n,* hypocritical *adj*

8. **manipulation** *n.*   Quietly moving or influencing people or things in order to get what you want

   Bob's **manipulation** of the boss's feelings led to his promotion.

   Parts of speech   manipulate *v,* manipulator *n,* manipulative *adj*

9. **rebel** *v.*   To go against an established system or authority

   The people of Ghurdia **rebelled** against the dictator and set up a new government.

Usage tips   *Rebel* works well in political contexts and in contexts of personal relationships.

Parts of speech   rebel *n*, rebellion *n*

10. **status quo** *n.*   The systems and conditions that exist now

Let's just maintain the **status quo** until we can think of a better way.

TOEFL Prep I   Find the word or phrase that is closest in meaning to each word in the left-hand column. Write the letter in the blank.

_____ 1. adolescent

_____ 2. conflict

_____ 3. delinquency

_____ 4. fringe

_____ 5. status quo

(a) not doing what you're supposed to

(b) clash; not fit together

(c) edge

(d) like a teenager

(e) current conditions

TOEFL Prep II   Complete each sentence by filling in the blank with the best word from the list. Change the form of the word if necessary. Use each word only once.

cause   hedonistic   hypocritically   manipulation   rebel

1. Senator Bond, who often lied to Congress, _____ called the president a liar.

2. Some monks criticized the well-fed, art-loving people of fifteenth-century Florence for being _____.

3. During the 1970s, college students fought for one _____ after another, from saving the whales to changing the government.

4. Even though it's illegal, _____ of lawmakers by rich companies is common.

5. It's natural for young people to _____ against society, but not with violence.

TOEFL Success   Read the passage to review the vocabulary you have learned. Answer the questions that follow.

Many *adolescents* and young adults go through a period when they *rebel* against what they perceive as an insincere world. Teens may take up *causes* such as radical environmentalism, protesting against the *status quo.* They may choose clothes that annoy their parents and associate with people from the *fringes* of society. This is a delicate period in a person's life, full of chances to make bad decisions that could lead to juvenile *delinquency* and even jail. **Conversely,** it can be a time of personal discovery that strengthens teens in a moral rejection of *hedonistic* lifestyles. At this age they may fearlessly speak up against *hypocritically* self-righteous authorities and against *manipulation* by the news media. These adolescent protests can lead to *conflicts* within families and communities, but stirring things up can also lead to serious reflection and positive change.

> *Bonus Structure—*
> *Conversely means*
> *"on the other*
> *hand."*

1. Which sentence best expresses the essential information of this passage?
   a. Teens are hedonistic and self-serving.
   b. Many teenagers are radical environmentalists.
   c. Adolescents often create conflicts in their communities.
   d. Teenage rebellion can cause problems, but it can be positive too.

2. According to the reading, what is one possible positive effect of teen rebellion?
   a. Adults might try to make positive changes.
   b. Teens may get in trouble with the police.
   c. Teens may become responsible adults later in life.
   d. Adults might imitate teens and also rebel.

Lesson 36   Social Rebels

TOEFL Prep I   1. d   2. b   3. a   4. c   5. e
TOEFL Prep II   1. hypocritically   2. hedonistic   3. cause
   4. manipulation   5. rebel
TOEFL Success   1. d   2. a

Painting and Sculpture

Target Words

1. abstract	6. intrinsic
2. context	7. perspective
3. depict	8. portrayal
4. dimension	9. realism
5. esthetically	10. spectrum

Definitions and Samples

1. **abstract** *adj.* Not concrete and realistic; not obviously related to every-day experience

   Abstract painting became popular partly because early photography was very realistic.

   Parts of speech abstraction *n*

2. **context** *n.* A larger environment that something fits into

   In the **context** of Soviet Russia, public art had to be about the triumph of communism and its leaders.

   Usage tips The preposition *in* often comes before *context*, and an *of* phrase often comes after it.

   Parts of speech contextualize *v*, contextual *adj*

3. **depict** *v.*   To show in pictures

Michelangelo's painting on the ceiling of the Sistine Chapel **depicts** nine scenes from the Bible.

Parts of speech   depiction *n*

4. **dimension** *n.*   A direction or surface along which something can be measured; an aspect

The three **dimensions** of physical objects are length, width, and depth.

One **dimension** of the problem is their long history of competition.

Parts of speech   dimensional *adj*

5. **esthetically** *adv.*   In a way that relates to beauty or appearance

The outside of the office building is **esthetically** pleasing, but the inside is dark and unpleasant.

Usage tips   *Esthetically* is often spelled with an "a" at the beginning: *aesthetically*.

Parts of speech   esthetic *n*, esthete *n*, esthetic *adj*

6. **intrinsic** *adj.*   Being part of the basic nature of something

Frequent elections are **intrinsic** to a democratic system.

Parts of speech   intrinsically *adv*

7. **perspective** *n.*   A way of seeing from a particular location; a way of thinking about something

From my **perspective,** the entire town can be seen through a set of large windows.

They held different **perspectives** on how to care for their aging parents.

8. **portrayal** *n.*   A description or drawing that reflects a certain point of view

Most **portrayals** of Abraham Lincoln emphasize his sense of humor and his honesty.

Usage tips   *Portrayal* is often followed by an *of* phrase to indicate what is being described.

Parts of speech   portray *v*

9. **realism** *n.*   A technique that tries to picture something as it really looks

 Realism was popular among seventeenth-century Flemish painters like Rembrandt van Rijn.

 Parts of speech   realist *n,* realistic *adj*

10. **spectrum** *n.*   A range of different things, usually colors

 Bart's colorful designs include every color of the **spectrum,** from deep blue to vibrant red.

 Usage tips   The phrase *the spectrum* frequently means "the colors that the human eye can see."

TOEFL Prep I   Find the word or phrase that is closest in meaning to each word in the left-hand column. Write the letter in the blank.

_____ 1. abstract	(a) to show
_____ 2. depict	(b) depiction
_____ 3. esthetically	(c) presenting an idea, not a realistic picture
_____ 4. perspective	(d) in a way that relates to beauty
_____ 5. portrayal	(e) way of seeing things from a certain place

TOEFL Prep II   Circle the word that best completes each sentence.

1. The materials that go into a work of art usually have little (abstract / intrinsic) value.
2. In the 1970s, artists known as "the Boston School" revived (realism / context) by rejecting abstract techniques and trying to capture the actual appearance of their subjects.
3. The colors of light that we can see are known as the visible (spectrum / perspective).

4. Medieval artists did not try to use (context / perspective) to give a sense of depth to their paintings.

5. The small, separate strokes of impressionist paintings give the works a dreamlike (portrayal / dimension).

TOEFL Success Read the passage to review the vocabulary you have learned. Answer the questions that follow.

Whether something is "art" is largely a matter of opinion. Art that most people consider to have no *intrinsic* value can contain a great treasure of ideas and invention to someone who sees something special in it. Styles in all the arts range over a wide *spectrum*. Some good art is *esthetically* unchallenging and easy to understand. Other works are strange forms, **totally** out of *context* to everyone but the artist. One artist's *portrayal* of an everyday object, such as a bouquet of flowers, may be grounded in *realism* and easily recognizable. Another painter's *depiction* of the same bouquet may be very *abstract,* resembling flowers only in the artist's mind. Regardless of the artist's approach, the best art reveals new *dimensions* of experience and looks at the world from a fresh *perspective.*

Bonus Structure— Totally *means* *"completely" or "in every way."*

1. Which sentence best expresses the essential information of this passage?
   a. Styles of art have changed throughout history.
   b. Realistic art has more meaning than abstract art.
   c. Esthetically pleasing art is too simple to contain much meaning.
   d. Works of art can mean different things, depending on one's perspective.

2. According to this reading, what is one big difference between abstract art and realistic art?
   a. Abstract art is harder to sell.
   b. Abstract art is harder to understand.
   c. Abstract art is harder to produce.
   d. Abstract art is harder to look at.

Lesson 37   Painting and Sculpture

TOEFL Prep I   1. c   2. a   3. d   4. e   5. b
TOEFL Prep II   1. intrinsic   2. realism   3. spectrum
    4. perspective   5. dimension
TOEFL Success   1. d   2. b

The Written Word

Target Words

1. advent
2. ambiguous
3. connotation
4. decipher
5. denote

6. illiterate
7. ingenious
8. inscription
9. phonetic
10. symbolic

Definitions and Samples

1. **advent** *n.* Coming; arrival

   The **advent** of the automobile greatly increased the demand for petroleum.

   Usage tips *Advent* is usually followed by an *of* phrase.

2. **ambiguous** *adj.* Having more than one possible meaning

   The sentence *It's hard to say* is **ambiguous,** with different meanings in different contexts.

   Parts of speech ambiguity *n,* ambiguously *adv*

3. **connotation** *n.* A meaning implied, not stated directly

   When my boss says, "Thank you," the **connotation** is that she's done talking and I should leave.

   Parts of speech connote *v*

4. **decipher** *v.*   To figure out the meaning, even though it is written in a
    code or an unknown language

    The Rosetta Stone helped archaeologists **decipher** ancient Egyptian
    writing.

    Usage tips   A cipher is a code or puzzle; *decipher* means "solve a
    puzzle written in code."

5. **denote** *v.*   To mean something clearly and directly

    An "X" next to a name on this list **denotes** a person who has been
    chosen for the soccer team.

    Parts of speech   denotation *n*

6. **illiterate** *adj.*   Unable to read

    In many villages nearly everyone was **illiterate** and unschooled, and
    the few who could read held great power.

    Parts of speech   illiterate *n,* illiteracy *n*

7. **ingenious** *adj.*   Very clever and imaginative

    Ann thought up an **ingenious** way to keep other people from acci-
    dentally taking her pens.

    Parts of speech   ingenuity *n,* ingeniously *adv*

8. **inscription** *n.*   Something written into a piece of rock or metal

    The **inscription** on my ring says "August 1," because that was the
    day of our wedding.

    Parts of speech   inscribe *v*

9. **phonetic** *adj.*   Related to the sounds in a language

    Children learning to write often make up **phonetic** spellings, based
    on the way a word sounds.

    Parts of speech   phonetics *n,* phonetically *adv*

10. **symbolic** *adj.*   Acting as a sign for some other thing or idea

   Since the 1970s, yellow ribbons have been **symbolic** of hope that someone will return from a dangerous situation.

   Usage tips   *Symbolic* is often followed by an *of* phrase indicating the meaning of a symbol.

   Parts of speech   symbolize *v*, symbol *n*, symbolically *adv*

TOEFL Prep I   Find the word or phrase that is closest in meaning to each word in the left-hand column. Write the letter in the blank.

_____ 1. advent	(a)	approach or arrival
_____ 2. decipher	(b)	newly invented in a clever way
_____ 3. ingenious	(c)	to figure out the meaning
_____ 4. inscription	(d)	related to spoken sounds
_____ 5. phonetic	(e)	something written into a hard surface

TOEFL Prep II   Complete each sentence by filling in the blank with the best word from the list. Change the form of the word if necessary. Use each word only once.

ambiguous   connotation   denote   illiterate   symbolic

1. If my father told me to be quiet, the _____ was "I have a headache."

2. The president's response, "Wait and see," was _____, meaning that perhaps he would take action, perhaps not.

3. In English writing, a mark called an apostrophe usually _____ a missing letter, as in *isn't* for *is not*.

4. A circle with a plus attached (♀) is _____ of "woman" and of the planet Venus.

5. Farley was a poor, _____ boy from a remote area who later taught himself to read and write.

TOEFL Success   Read the passage to review the vocabulary you have learned. Answer the questions that follow.

Johannes Gutenberg's *ingenious* use of movable type in his printing press had a wide range of effects on European societies. **Most obviously,** readers no longer had to *decipher* odd handwriting, with *ambiguous* lettering, in order to read a written work. Gutenberg gave each letter standard forms, a move that had *connotations* far beyond the printing business. The *inscriptions* on tombstones and roadside mileposts, for example, could now be standardized. The cost of books decreased. Even *illiterate* people benefited indirectly from the *advent* of this invention, as the general level of information in society increased. However, Gutenberg's press was of limited use for languages that used picture-like symbols for writing instead of a *phonetic* system. Systems of *symbolic* pictographs, each of which *denotes* a word, require many thousands of characters to be cast into lead type by the printer. Phonetic systems, like the Latin alphabet, use the same few characters, recombined in thousands of ways to make different words.

> *Bonus Structure—* **Most obviously** *introduces an easy-to-see effect and implies that less-clear effects will come later.*

1. According to this reading, how did the invention of the printing press benefit illiterate people?

    a. It helped them learn to read.
    b. It raised the level of information in a society.
    c. It lowered the cost of books.
    d. It saved them from having to read ambiguous handwriting.

2. Why was Gutenberg's press not very practical for languages that use picture-like symbols?

    a. because character-based languages are made of pictographs
    b. because phonetic alphabets are clearer
    c. because there are too many characters to make movable type for each one
    d. because Gutenberg was European, so he didn't know any character-based languages

Lesson 38   The Written Word

TOEFL Prep I   1. a   2. c   3. b   4. e   5. d

TOEFL Prep II   1. connotation   2. ambiguous   3. denote
   4. symbolic   5. literate

TOEFL Success   1. b   2. c

Entertainment

Target Words

1. amateurish
2. cast
3. charismatic
4. gala
5. hilarious
6. improvisation
7. incompetent
8. medium
9. skit
10. zeal

Definitions and Samples

1. **amateurish** *adj.*   Not good enough to be the work of professionals

   Whoever painted this room did an **amateurish** job, with all sorts of uneven edges.

   Parts of speech   amateur *n,* amateurishly *adv*

2. **cast** *n.*   The group of actors in a play, movie, television show, etc.

   Some viewers mistakenly start thinking that a TV show's **cast** members are really the characters they play.

   Usage tips   In U.S. English, *cast* is singular. In some other varieties of English it is plural.

   Parts of speech   cast *v*

3. **charismatic** *adj.*   Extremely attractive and charming

   Because of the sparkle in his eye and his confident style, John F. Kennedy was a **charismatic** leader.

   Parts of speech   charisma *n,* charismatically *adv*

4. **gala** *adj.*   Expensive, elaborately arranged, and full of celebration

   A college graduation party should be a **gala** affair, not a backyard barbecue.

   Usage tips   *Gala* is somewhat old-fashioned, far more common in print than in speech.

   Parts of speech   gala *n*

5. **hilarious** *adj.*   Very funny

   In my opinion, the most **hilarious** character on television was Basil Fawlty.

   Parts of speech   hilarity *n*

6. **improvisation** *n.*   Inventing a solution to an unexpected problem

   Boy Scouts take pride in their **improvisation** when faced with trouble during a camping trip.

   Parts of speech   improvise *v*, improvisational *adj*

7. **incompetent** *adj.*   Unskilled; lacking the ability to perform a task

   Because we hired an **incompetent** builder to replace our roof, we now have leaks everywhere.

   Usage tips   Usually, *incompetent* implies that someone tries to do something but fails.

   Parts of speech   incompetence *n*, incompetently *adv*

8. **medium** *n.*   A channel or way for a meaning to be expressed

   Watercolor art is often considered childish, but some artists have achieved great things working in that **medium.**

   Usage tips   The plural of *medium* is *media.*

9. **skit** *n.*   A short, informal play

   Marnie and Chris spent a long time practicing their **skit** for the school show.

10. **zeal** *n.* Enthusiasm; a deep determination to do well

Unfortunately, Tom's **zeal** to become a rock star distracted him from his studies.

Usage tips *Zeal* is often followed by *to* plus a verb or by a *for* phrase.

Parts of speech zealot *n,* zealous *adj*

TOEFL Prep I Find the word or phrase that is closest in meaning to each word in the left-hand column. Write the letter in the blank.

_____ 1. amateurish   (a) group of people in a movie

_____ 2. cast   (b) very funny

_____ 3. hilarious   (c) unable to perform a task

_____ 4. incompetent   (d) enthusiasm

_____ 5. zeal   (e) not like professionals

TOEFL Prep II Complete each sentence by filling in the blank with the best word from the list. Change the form of the word if necessary. Use each word only once.

charismatic   gala   improvisation   medium   skit

1. The sixth-grade class put on a little _____ about Thanksgiving Day.

2. The year ended with a _____ celebration featuring a professional orchestra.

3. Gena's skills at _____ saved the play when she forgot her real lines.

4. Television is a passive _____ because it demands no input from the viewer.

5. Movie stars that are especially _____ often take advantage of their charm to go into politics.

TOEFL Success   Read the passage to review the vocabulary you have learned. Answer the questions that follow.

When the artistic *medium* of theater falls into the hands of college students, the results can be unpredictable. At one college, we saw Shakespeare's *Hamlet* done as musical theater. The idea was bad to start out with, and the actual play was *amateurish,* bordering on *incompetent.* The *cast* did not understand the tragic power of the play. Their *improvisation* when they forgot their lines was silly and inappropriate. The costumes and set design looked homemade, like something

Bonus Structure—
However indicates
a change in focus.

from an elementary-school *skit.* Three months later, **however,** this same group of students did a great job with the comedy *A Midsummer Night's Dream.* Surprisingly enough, the actors were *charismatic,* played their parts with *zeal,* and achieved a *hilarious* result. It was no *gala* event, but we still felt that it was one of the best performances we had seen.

1. What word best describes the author's opinion of the student performance of *Hamlet?*
    a. incompetent
    b. charismatic
    c. hilarious
    d. full of zeal

2. What is the author's opinion of student performances in general?
    a. Students should not perform Shakespeare's plays.
    b. Sometimes student productions are good, and other times they are not.
    c. All student shows are amateurish.
    d. Student performances should be gala events.

Lesson 39   Entertainment

TOEFL Prep I   1. e   2. a   3. b   4. c   5. d
TOEFL Prep II   1. skit   2. gala   3. improvisation   4. medium
       5. charismatic
TOEFL Success   1. a   2. b

Risky Fashions

Target Words

1. bulk
2. capricious
3. cumbersome
4. exotic
5. inhibit

6. minimum
7. striking
8. trend
9. vanity
10. vulnerable

Definitions and Samples

1. **bulk** *n.* Largeness and a heavy appearance

   The **bulk** of Kevin's athletic body was too great for one small chair, so he sat on a bench.

   Parts of speech bulky *adj*

2. **capricious** *adj.* Moving unpredictably from one thing to another

   Your college studies will go on too long if you make **capricious** jumps from one major to another.

   Usage tips *Capricious* comes from a Latin word meaning "goat" and implies a motion like the jumping of a goat.

   Parts of speech capriciousness *n,* capriciously *adv*

3. **cumbersome** *adj.* Difficult to wear or carry because of weight or shape

   To make it to the top of the mountain before dark, the hikers dumped their **cumbersome** tent.

4. **exotic** *adj.*   Interesting or unusual because of coming from a faraway place

I walked into the restaurant and smelled the **exotic** aromas of Malaysian spices.

Parts of speech   exoticism *n,* exotically *adv*

5. **inhibit** *v.*   To discourage or to slow down

This lotion will **inhibit** the itching caused by mosquito bites.

Parts of speech   inhibition *n*

6. **minimum** *n.*   The smallest possible amount or level

The **minimum** for being accepted to Cavill University is a score of 60 on the test.

Parts of speech   minimize *v,* minimum *adj,* minimal *adj,* minimally *adv*

7. **striking** *adj.*   Very noticeable; easily attracting attention

Gordon had a **striking** new attitude after he learned self-discipline at the army academy.

Usage tips   *Striking* comes from a verb that means "to hit."

Parts of speech   strike *v,* strikingly *adv*

8. **trend** *n.*   A movement in one direction or a widespread change in fashion

The **trend** among some young men is to wear their caps with the bill off to one side.

Parts of speech   trend *v,* trendy *adj*

9. **vanity** *n.*   An excessive concern for one's appearance

Mark's **vanity** led him to spend far too much money on haircuts and new clothes.

Parts of speech   vain *adj*

10. **vulnerable** *adj.*   Exposed to possible harm

Babies and very old people are especially **vulnerable** to the new disease.

Usage tips   *Vulnerable* is often followed by a *to* phrase.

Parts of speech   vulnerability *n*, vulnerably *adv*

TOEFL Prep I   Find the word or phrase that is closest in meaning to the opposite of each word in the left-hand column. Write the letter in the blank.

_____ 1. capricious   (a) encourage
_____ 2. exotic   (b) maximum
_____ 3. inhibit   (c) ordinary
_____ 4. minimum   (d) predictable
_____ 5. vulnerable   (e) well protected

TOEFL Prep II   Circle the word that best completes the sentence.

1. The (trend / bulk) of his sweater made him look fatter than he really was.
2. Some analysts see a relationship between fashion (trends / vanity) and the ups and down of the economy.
3. The outfits worn by firefighters are (vulnerable / cumbersome) and heavy.
4. Her necklace was especially (cumbersome / striking) because of the diamonds it contained.
5. (Vanity / Bulk) led my grandfather to dye his hair and to dress like someone 40 years younger.

TOEFL Success   Read the passage to review the vocabulary you have learned. Answer the questions that follow.

The fashion industry encourages people to spend far too much time and money on clothes. **It's natural for** humans to use clothing as a mark of

Bonus Structure—
It's natural for
introduces an
aspect of fashion
that's not bad, but
it implies that an
"unnatural" aspect
will come next.

belonging to a group and to try to keep up with style *trends*. The fashion industry exploits this natural desire and turns it into a *capricious,* impractical, and expensive rush from one style to another. For example, in one recent year, fashion did an abrupt about-face. Early in the year, fashionable outfits showed a *minimum* amount of fabric and a maximum amount of skin. By late summer, famous fashion designers were drowning people in *bulky, cumbersome* outfits that looked five sizes too big. *Vanity inhibits* people from looking realistically at *exotic* clothing fads. A *striking* new style catches their eye, they look at the clothes they're wearing, and they are suddenly *vulnerable* to the manipulation of the fashion industry.

1. Which word best describes the fashion industry, according to the author?

   a. striking
   b. minimum
   c. capricious
   d. vulnerable

2. What is one reason people buy the latest fashions, according to the author?

   a. Because they want to feel like they are part of the group.
   b. Because they enjoy spending money.
   c. Because the fashion world is bizarre.
   d. Because their clothes from last year don't fit.

Lesson 40   Risky Fashions

TOEFL Prep I   1. d   2. c   3. a   4. b   5. e
TOEFL Prep II   1. bulk   2. trends   3. cumbersome   4. striking
     5. Vanity
TOEFL Success   1. c   2. a

400 Must-Have Words for the TOEFL

abandon

abduction

abstract

accumulate

accuracy

accuse

acquire

acquisition

adapt

addictive

adjacent

adjust

adolescent

advent

adversely

advocate

affection

affluence

aggravate

aggregate

agnostic

allegedly

allegiance

allocate

amateurish

ambiguous

amend

analyze

ancestral

anesthesia

animism

annex

anomaly

anticipate

antipathy

apex

apprehend

arbitrary

arrogantly

artillery

ascertain

assail

assess

asset

assimilate

associate

astrological

atheist

augment

authority

battle

be inclined to

berate
biased
bitterly
bond
bribery
bulk
burden
bureaucratic

candidate
capricious
cartel
cast
catastrophic
cause
cease
certifiably
charismatic
chronologically
circulate
civil
clique
coalition
coerce
cohesion
coincide
collapse
collide
combustion
commodity
compensate
complex
complication
component
compress
concentrated
condemn
confide
conflict
connotation

conquest
consciously
consequence
constraint
contamination
contemplate
contemptuous
contest
context
contrary
convey
convict
core
corrode
counter
cremation
cultivation
cumbersome
cure
curriculum
cynically

de facto
decipher
decline
decrepit
degrade
deify
delinquency
denominator
denote
deny
depict
deplete
derive
descendant
despise
despondent
detain
detection

deviant

devise

devotion

dilemma

dimension

diminish

discretely

discriminate

disease

dispose of

distill

distinctly

distort

diverse

divination

domesticate

dynamic

ecclesiastical

election

elementally

elite

emission

engender

enterprising

entrepreneurial

equity

erode

erudite

eruption

esthetically

evade

evidence

evolve

exalt

exclusive

exotic

expeditiously

exploit

exponentially

extinction

extract

famine

fatally

feasibly

feature

fertilize

flood

fluctuate

folklore

forensics

fortify

fossilize

fringe

gala

gap

generation

grotesque

guilty

gut

haggle

haunt

hazardous

hedonistic

hierarchy

hilarious

horror

humiliation

hypocritically

hypothesize

illiterate

impact

impair

implant

implement

implicate

implicitly

impoverish

improvisation

in common

in the trenches

inaugurate

incentive

incompetent

indisputable

industrious

inference

infinitesimal

inflation

ingenious

inherent

inheritance

inhibit

inject

innovative

inquiry

inscription

installation

integrally

integrity

intensify

intentionally

interdict

intermediary

intervene

intrepid

intrinsic

intrusively

intuitively

invasive

invoke

irrigation

jointly

juxtapose

kin

lease

legitimate

liability

longitude

loyal

luxury

maintenance

manipulation

marginal

maximize

meditate

medium

merchant

merit

migration

milieu

minimum

misconception

mobilize

modify

net

nobility

notion

nucleus

obese

objectively

obnoxious

obtain

offense

oppress

Orwellian

overlap

paradigm
parallel
parochial
passion
paternal
peer
per capita
permeate
persevere
persist
perspective
phantom
phonetic
photosynthesis
physical
pious
piracy
plunge
policy
poll
portrayal
potent
precipitation
predicament
prejudiced
prestige
prevailing
prevalent
privileged
procedure
process
prognosis
proliferation
promote
proportion
proportionately
proprietor
prosper
prototype
proximity
psychic

rank
rate
ratio
realism
rebel
recede
reciprocity
reconciliation
reform
regulate
relic
reservoir
residual
resign
resist
retain
retrieve
reward
rigor
rite
ritually
roster
rotate

sacrifice
safeguard
saga
scandal
scar
secular
seep
seize
self-perpetuating
sentiment
sequence
severely
shame
shrink
shuttle
sibling

simulation
skit
smuggle
solar
sole
solidarity
source
spectrum
stable
status quo
stigmatize
strategic
striking
structure
subsidy
subtly
surveillance
survive
suspect
suspend
suspicious
symbolic

tangible
terminal
tolerate

trend
trigger

unleash
unmask

vanish
vanity
vein
verdict
versus
vestige
villainy
violation
vitriolic
vulnerable

willing
witness
working class
wound

zeal

About the Authors

LYNN STAFFORD-YILMAZ has taught ESL for 15 years and is the author of several popular ESL books.

LAWRENCE J. ZWIER teaches at Michigan State University and is the author of numerous general interest and ESL books, including *Building Academic Vocabulary*.